THE SLOW PROFESSOR

Challenging the Culture of Speed in the Academy

Maggie Berg and Barbara K. Seeber
With a New Foreword by Stefan Collini

If there is one sector of society that should be cultivating deep thought in itself and others, it is academia. Yet the corporatization of the contemporary university has sped up the clock, demanding increased speed and efficiency from faculty regardless of the consequences for education and scholarship.

In *The Slow Professor*, Maggie Berg and Barbara K. Seeber discuss how adopting the principles of the Slow movement in academic life can counter this erosion of humanistic education. Focusing on the individual faculty member and his or her own professional practice, Berg and Seeber present both an analysis of the culture of speed in the academy and ways of alleviating stress while improving teaching, research, and collegiality. *The Slow Professor* is a must-read for anyone in academia concerned about the frantic pace of contemporary university life.

MAGGIE BERG is a professor in the Department of English at Queen's University. A winner of the Chancellor A. Charles Baillie Award for Teaching Excellence, she held the Queen's Chair of Teaching and Learning from 2009 to 2012.

BARBARA K. SEEBER is a professor in the Department of English at Brock University. She received the Brock Faculty of Humanities Award for Excellence in Teaching in 2014.

"I love this book. Mentors should give it to newly hired faculty members. Advisors should buy it for their graduating PhDs. Individual faculty should read it to reclaim some of their sanity."

Nancy Chick, University Chair in Teaching and Learning
and Academic Director of the Taylor Institute
for Teaching and Learning, University of Calgary

"I read this book with the intensity and engagement that I read a novel. It's a fresh and insightful study that reaches out to readers with wisdom as well as information."

Teresa Mangum, Director of the Obermann Center
for Advanced Studies, University of Iowa

"In *The Slow Professor*, authors Maggie Berg and Barbara Seeber neither describe nor endorse procrastination and lethargy ... They see the need and advocate for deliberative, imaginative, and reflective thought as definitive of a professor's work and life. Creativity and contemplation, they understand, can't be multitasked ... It is reminiscent of the era of consciousness-raising that grounded second-wave feminism a half-century ago ... It gently and good-humouredly reassures the novice and the veteran alike that their fears, their feelings of futility, and their fretful excursions into sometimes damaging self-criticism are not entirely their fault. The book is aspirational and redemptive."

Howard A. Doughty, *CAUT Bulletin*

"What Maggie Berg and Barbara Seeber are doing in *The Slow Professor* is protesting against the 'corporatization of the contemporary university,' and reminding us of a kind of 'good' selfishness; theirs is a self-help book that recognises the fact that an institution can only ever be as healthy as the sum of its parts"

Emma Rees, *Times Higher Education*

"It isn't too late, Berg and Seeber write, to reclaim a more sane and deliberate rhythm of work; and to reclaim pleasure in teaching; to reclaim collegiality ... It is a welcome part of a crucial conversation."

Rachel Hadas, *Times Literary Supplement*

" ... While it's already raised some eyebrows as an example of 'tenured privilege,' it's at once an important addition and possible antidote to the growing literature on the corporatization of the university ... What makes Berg and Seeber's argument unique, however, is that they reject the 'crisis' language that dominates the many books that have come before ... Instead, *Slow Professor* proposes with some optimism that professors ... have the power to change the direction of the university by becoming the eye of the storm, working deliberately and thoughtfully in ways that somehow now seem taboo."

Colleen Flaherty, *Inside Higher Education*

"Maggie Berg and Barbara K. Seeber's *The Slow Professor: Challenging the Culture of Speed in the Academy* is a much-discussed manifesto that has launched a vitally needed conversation on the importance – and pleasures – of protecting open enquiry from the frantic pace of the modern academic assembly line."

Susan Prentice, *Times Higher Education, Books of the Year 2016*

The Slow Professor

Challenging the Culture of Speed in the Academy

MAGGIE BERG AND BARBARA K. SEEBER

UNIVERSITY OF TORONTO PRESS
Toronto Buffalo London

© University of Toronto Press 2016
Toronto Buffalo London
www.utppublishing.com
Printed in Canada

Reprinted in paperback 2017

ISBN 978-1-4426-4556-1 (cloth)
ISBN 978-1-4875-2185-1 (paper)

Library and Archives Canada Cataloguing in Publication

Berg, Maggie, author
The slow professor : challenging the culture of speed in the academy/
Maggie Berg and Barbara K. Seeber.

Includes bibliographical references and index.
ISBN 978-1-4426-4556-1 (cloth)   ISBN 978-1-4875-2185-1 (paperback)

1. College teaching.   2. Education, Higher – Philosophy.
3. Slow life movement.   4. Time management.   I. Seeber, Barbara
Karolina, 1968–, author   II. Title.

LB2331.B45 2016   378.1'25   C2015-907570-X

University of Toronto Press acknowledges the financial assistance to
its publishing program of the Canada Council for the Arts and the
Ontario Arts Council, an agency of the Government of Ontario.

Canada Council   Conseil des Arts
for the Arts   du Canada

ONTARIO ARTS COUNCIL
CONSEIL DES ARTS DE L'ONTARIO
an Ontario government agency
un organisme du gouvernement de l'Ontario

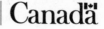

Funded by the   Financé par le
Government   gouvernement
of Canada   du Canada   Canadä

Contents

Foreword

It has taken me a long time to write this foreword. But then, writing usually does take a long time, I find – certainly long when compared to the brevity and unsatisfactoriness of the outcome. However, it may be a mistake, a representative and revealing mistake, to concentrate on the "outcome." Writing is a complex activity, and quite a lot happens along the way, including discovering what we really think. In the present case, for example, I have also found myself doing some background reading, brooding on the functions of a foreword to a book which already does a good job of introducing itself to its readers, and reflecting on the differences between "classroom teaching" (the default form of university teaching assumed in North America) and lectures, seminars, and tutorials (the main familiar modes in the UK). As it happens, I have also made quite a lot of coffee, been running, imagined conversations with the book's authors (whom I've never met), and tidied my study. I concede that a more disciplined writer might have dispensed with some of these elements, though I'm a little suspicious of those aspects of "discipline" which are self-punitive to the point where unremitting toil becomes a perverse psychic satisfaction in itself. Still, these or other comparable ingredients are part of most writers' experience of writing, and one of the many valuable recommendations in this book is that we academics should, collectively, talk to each other more about how we actually spend our time, with all the anxieties, displacements, and failures that involves, rather than presenting ourselves as the overachieving writing robots whom most systems of assessment seem designed to reward.

Such systems are supposed to stimulate productivity, though the truth is that one of the main obstacles to genuine intellectual productivity in contemporary academia is that most scholars publish too much. I do not say that they *write* too much: "write more and publish less" is a valuable injunction, encouraging us to explore our thinking more, and only to publish when we are sure we have something worth saying. In the humanities (I cannot speak from experience for other disciplines), we largely think by writing – or, rather, by trying to write and thus discovering that we don't quite know what we think. Similarly, re-writing is not chiefly a matter of buffing up already polished prose, but of coming to think a little more clearly and exactly. It all takes time.

Taking our time, taking as much time as it takes, taking back our time – these are among Maggie Berg and Barbara Seeber's main recommendations in this timely book. As they recognize, life in contemporary universities has become so hurried and harried that the processes that generate this frenzy of ostentatious busyness now threaten to frustrate the purposes for which such institutions exist. Spending time applying for grants to do research rather than actually doing research; spending time reporting that the outcomes of a course conformed to the guidelines rather than thinking about how to teach the course next year; spending time sitting on committees that report on how many grant applications were successful and how many course outcomes satisfactory rather than exchanging ideas with colleagues – these are all symptoms of a system in which managerialist imperatives displace the activities they are meant to be supporting.

Berg and Seeber are, of course, not alone in their diagnosis of this malady, as their numerous references to other scholars make clear (perhaps I had better explain that I agreed to write this foreword before I discovered what generous things they say about some of my own work on the topic). But they may be unusual in concentrating on the existential condition of the individual professor and what she or he can do to combat this malaise. They give eloquent expression to the way in which the misconceived imposition of the nostrums of the business consultants results in the hollowed-out subjectivity of the contemporary academic, a form of harassed self-estrangement that perfectly replicates the model of the neoliberal economic agent, restlessly seeking to maximize personal advantage in a situation of ceaseless competition.

Yet even if contemporary universities were not largely run as boot-camps for pliant self-improvers, there would still be a tension between the demands of everyday tasks and the conditions that encourage intellectual creativity. We are all familiar with the narrowed, instrumental focus that comes with efficiency mode. We tick items off actual or mental lists; we are highly organized, very professional, and impressively quick. Letters of reference, revisions to reading lists, synopses of next term's lectures, reports to publishers, internal memos: each touch of the "send" key ramps up our sense of achievement. And then there is the ur-task, the daily Sisyphean struggle to clear our inboxes – a task which, in its combination of disagreeableness and meritoriousness, is the electronic equivalent of scrubbing the kitchen floor. (Full disclosure: my inbox currently contains 1762 messages, though that mainly indicates that I am an intermittent and indecisive filer, not that I am supremely indifferent or exceptionally popular.) But efficiency mode is not conducive to having new or worthwhile thoughts. That usually requires those periods of moody inactivity, or apparent inactivity, a slightly depressive state in which self-reproach and free-association are conjoined in a way more reminiscent of sexual frustration than of inbox-zapping. Berg and Seeber speak up for inactivity, or apparent inactivity, and they speak up for speaking about these states to each other. Such exchanges are a way of pooling our resources, of collectively identifying the conditions conducive to doing good work.

Of course, the authors recognize that the world around universities has speeded up as well, and there are limits to how far any individual or group can seal themselves off from the effects of the Internet, mobile phones, 24-hour rolling news, social media, and the state of living in what has been nicely termed

"data smog" – a condition also described as "self-induced ADD."
However, just as "think globally, act locally" is good counsel for
activism in general, so those of us who are academics can only
start from where we are and do what we can do. But that, as
Berg and Seeber show, is still quite a lot. Many of the steps they
recommend are instances of what I call the "double consciousness" which academics have got used to living with over recent
decades. We know that many of the exactions of the audit culture and associated managerialism are misconceived and damaging, but we also know that there has to be at least a minimal
show of compliance with them. So, even as we go through the
motions of squeezing our activities into a series of boxes designed by people with no real understanding of the activities
themselves, we also keep alive a different vocabulary and a different way of judging value (one that begins by recognizing that
it has to be *judged* and not *measured*). And we do this – Berg and
Seeber are recommending that we become more self-conscious
and explicit about it – in part by talking to each other and to
our students in ways that do justice to the nature of open-ended
intellectual enquiry or the expansion of intellectual horizons,
or even just to the importance of a well-turned sentence that
has not been dismembered into the bureaucratic burping of
ungrammatical bullet points.

Beyond this, they urge changes that have more to do with
ethos and character than with isolable procedures. They remind
us of the need to find pleasure in doing what we do – indeed, to
remember that we do it better when we take pleasure in it. And
they exhort us to be less solitary and self-protective, to be more
open-handed with our ideas, our support, and, yes, our time.
Building real collegiality, as opposed to meeting the obligations
of "service" in a grudging, CV-burnishing way, involves not just
labour but generosity of spirit and a willingness to expose one's
own frailties. Their book has elements of a radical manifesto and
elements of a self-help manual, as well as being a short hymn to
intellectual friendship. It encourages rather than berates, while
its very existence exemplifies what it recommends.

When first published in the spring of 2016, *The Slow Professor* met with an enthusiastic reception, being reviewed more widely and more positively than, it would seem, its authors or its publisher had expected. Predictably, both its argument and its success have provoked some below-the-line sneering along the lines of "pampered academics whingeing about having to work for a living," though in fact Berg and Seeber's exhortation to us to think harder about what is really valuable in teaching, scholarship, and collegiality arguably represents a more, rather than less, strenuous ethic than that endorsed by conventional career imperatives. (I ought to make clear that I shall probably never know whether this foreword comes in for its share of similar Internet sneering, since I long ago discovered that not reading such online comment threads is one of the easiest ways to save time and avoid being led into despair about the human race.)

The Slow Professor is an attractively short book, but whatever you do, don't read it too quickly. And don't just read it: give it to friends, talk about it with people, try to do what it suggests. In your own time ...

Stefan Collini
September 2016

Preface

Western civilization teaches us that displays of busyness are useful and impressive.

Boice, First-Order Principles, 38

Moment by moment, when we're rushed, we're simply not the people we're capable of being.

Rettig 74

The Slow Professor draws on a number of genres. We have been influenced by the literature on the corporatization of higher education, empirical studies which document the harmful effects of stress and loneliness on physiological and psychological health, popular self-help discourse which emphasizes the importance of work-life balance, and, of course, the key texts of the Slow movement. We have learned a great deal from these schools of thought, and while our book shares some of their characteristics, it is unique in its blending of philosophical, political, and pragmatic concerns. Our book is more optimistic than works on the corporate university, more political and historicized than self-help, and more academically focused than those on stress and the Slow movement. Indeed, this is the first book to date which extends Slow principles to academia.

Both of us are literary critics, and writing this book nudged us out of our comfort zone. It required us to unlearn parts of our academic training; doing so, paradoxically, allowed us to remember vital aspects of academic life which are in danger of becoming relics of the past. The argument of *The Slow Professor* is supported by empirical studies conducted in fields such as sociology, medicine, information science, and labour studies, and it is also rooted in personal experience. While we worried at times that the book was too personal, we began to see that the inclusion of testimonies was crucial to the project and inextricably linked to its politics. Magda Lewis, in her article "More Than Meets the Eye: The Under Side of the Corporate Culture of Higher Education and Possibilities for a New Feminist Critique," reminds us that anecdotes are "a fundamental prerequisite to developing new understandings concerning the workings of larger political discourses and structures" (12). The purpose of the testimony, then, is not to reveal "individual characteristics" but to "amplify the political context that make[s] these events possible and ... provide the ground from which a collective conversation may begin about current social, political and intellectual life in the academy" (15). Moreover, as a recent article in the *Guardian Higher Education Network* indicates, "while anecdotal accounts multiply, mental health issues in academia are little-researched and hard data is thin on the ground" (Shaw and Ward). And given this "thinness" of "hard data," personal narratives can guide our thinking, our actions, and further research. We took a lesson from Marc Bekoff's comment about the emerging science on animal behaviour: "the plural of anecdote is data" (*Animal Studies Reader* 76). The testimony not only reflects our feminist approach and the current state of research on the topic, but also seeks to shed light on academic experiences which we believe are common, yet unacknowledged. Like Stefan Collini's *What Are Universities For?*, a book we greatly admire, we hope to "bring the reader to focus on and recognise something hitherto neglected, misdescribed, undervalued, or suppressed," and, like Collini, we believe that "the process of recognition is always in part an appeal to something which the reader, at some level, already knows" (xiii). Our personal stories, then, complement the data that is accumulating and the overall point of our book, which is to foster greater openness about the ways in which the corporate university affects our professional practice and well-being.

We hope this book will serve as an intervention. Given that this is our aim, we, at times, adopt the tone of a manifesto. At points, we are deliberately schematic in nature, identifying, in broad strokes, the forces at work in the contemporary university which jeopardize the long-honoured aims of higher education, as well as suggesting a model of resistance. *The Slow Professor* is a call to action and, as such, it is idealistic in nature. While our Slow Professor Manifesto (appended to this preface) has grown out of sustained scholarly work as well as personal reflection, it offers, in distilled form, a counter-identity, which we may claim, to the beleaguered, managed, frantic, stressed, and demoralized professor who is the product of the corporatization of higher education.

It was a careful choice on our part for our book not to grow into a 300-page scholarly tome our colleagues would likely be too busy to read. Our guiding principles were for *The Slow Professor* to be useful, accessible to a variety of disciplines, and affirming. While we acknowledge the systemic inequities in the university, a slow approach is potentially relevant across the spectrum of academic positions. Those of us in tenured positions, given the protection that we enjoy, have an obligation to try to improve in our own ways the working climate for all of us. We are concerned that the bar is being continually raised for each generation of faculty, so the book is also addressed to graduate students.

∽

The Slow Professor Manifesto

We are Slow Professors. We believe that adopting the principles of Slow into our professional practice is an effective way to alleviate work stress, preserve humanistic education, and resist the corporate university. The Slow Movement – originating in

Slow Food – challenges the frantic pace and standardization of contemporary culture. While slowness has been celebrated in architecture, urban life, and personal relations, it has not yet found its way into education. Yet, if there is one sector of society which should be cultivating deep thought, it is academic teachers. Corporatization has compromised academic life and sped up the clock. The administrative university is concerned above all with efficiency, resulting in a time crunch and making those of us subjected to it feel powerless. Talking about professors' stress is not self-indulgent; *not* talking about it plays into the corporate model.

In the corporate university, power is transferred from faculty to managers, economic justifications dominate, and the familiar "bottom line" eclipses pedagogical and intellectual concerns. Slow Professors advocate deliberation over acceleration. We need time to think, and so do our students. Time for reflection and open-ended inquiry is not a luxury but is crucial to what we do.

The language of crisis dominates the literature on the corporate university, urging us to act before it is too late. We are more optimistic, believing that resistance is alive and well. We envisage Slow Professors acting purposefully, cultivating emotional and intellectual resilience. By taking the time for reflection and dialogue, the Slow Professor takes back the intellectual life of the university.

Introduction

The caricature of the professor as a kindly, befuddled person with too much time on his hands bears about the same relationship to current reality as that of the newspaper reporter who, press badge in his fedora, exposes the wrongdoing of bad guys.

Pocklington and Tupper 51

This book began in a series of telephone conversations about coping with our academic jobs. Not reading an email sent by the department chair at 10:45 p.m. until the next morning led one of us into paroxysms of guilt about not working hard enough. Being asked to vet essays for a prize within ten days (without advance notice) prompted a discussion between us about when it is OK to say "no." Reading Carl Honoré's *In Praise of Slow* turned our desire to be less harried into a philosophical and political commitment to shift our sense of time. Honoré documents the benefits of extending the principles of Slow Food to other areas of our lives: architecture, medicine, sex, work, leisure, and child rearing. His inclusion in the last chapter of quotations from Dean Harry Lewis's open letter to Harvard undergraduates entitled "Slow Down: Getting More out of Harvard by Doing Less" (246–8) left us hungering for more. Our telephone conversations became more upbeat as we generated strategies to alleviate our time stress which ranged from checking email at noon to rethinking what we mean by coverage in a course. One day, one of us laughingly observed, "We should write this down," and the other responded, "We *should* write this down."

While we were unflaggingly playing therapist with each other, we came across the first-ever national survey on occupational stress conducted by the Canadian Association of University Teachers (CAUT) in 2007. The results – which are statistically representative (Catano et al. 8) – are based on 1470 participants from fifty-six universities across Canada and concur with previous studies in the UK and Australia. Ironically, it was liberating to learn from the Australian study that stress in academia exceeds that found in the general population (Catano et al. 7). We realized we were not alone. Particularly compelling was the significant impact of stress on psychological and physical health: "a relatively large number ... experienced a substantial number of physical (22.1%) and psychological (23.5%) health symptoms, and used stress-related medication (21.8%) over the past year" (Catano et al. 22). While there were differences according to gender, age, faculty rank, employment status, and language, the conclusion is that stress levels are "very high" overall (Catano et al. 38). It turns out we were not constitutionally weak or unsuited for the profession. Reading the survey was like opening a window. We shifted our thinking from "what is wrong with us?" to "what is wrong with the academic system?"

We did not make this shift overnight. Academic training includes induction into a culture of scholarly individualism and intellectual mastery; to admit to struggle undermines our professorial identity. The academy as a whole has been reticent in acknowledging its stress; to talk about the body and emotion goes against the grain of an institution that privileges the mind and reason. Furthermore, the long-standing perception of professors as a leisured class has produced a defensive culture of guilt and overwork. We are busy countering the widely held notion of the ivory tower. How many of us find that we snap in the grocery store when we have to explain yet again, "No, I don't have four months off in the summer"? Many non-academics would agree with Inspector Morse's characterization of professorial life:

"Once you're taken into the university's bosom ... you are preserved, like Sleeping Beauty, in a rarified atmosphere of hot air
and alcohol. Aging is unknown." We wish. It is not just that non-
academics don't understand what we do. The notion of the leisured professor is actively propagated; according to CareerCast
– widely disseminated in the mainstream media – being a professor was ranked as the least stressful occupation in 2013 and the
fourth least stressful in 2014. The reality, as William Deresiewicz
summarizes, is that "academic labor is becoming like every other
part of the American workforce: cowed, harried, docile, disem-
powered," but "the stereotype of the lazy academic is, like that of
the welfare queen, a politically useful myth" (par. 24).

In the current global context – in which universities are faced
more than ever with justifying their existence – to speak of professors' stress might appear self-indulgent. Indeed, some colleagues have suggested that we stop whining, while others have
described our project as brave. These opposing responses artic-
ulate our own internal dialogues. Being an academic has privileges not enjoyed by the majority of the workforce: job security
provided by the tenure system; flexibility of hours and the
changing rhythms of the academic year; and the opportunity to
think, create, and pass on our enthusiasms to others. We wanted
to become professors because of the joy of intellectual discovery, the beauty of literary texts, and the radical potential of new
ideas. These ideals are realizable, even in today's beleaguered
institution, although the ever-increasing casualization of labour
makes them harder to attain for many of us. Even the privileges
of tenure have a downside. Flexibility of hours can translate into
working all the time, particularly because academic work by its
very nature is never done. Our responses to student papers
could always be fuller; our reading of scholarly literature could
always be more up-to-date; and our books could always be more
exhaustive. These self-expectations are escalated by the additional external pressures of the changing academic culture. In
the past two decades, our work has changed due to the rise in
contractual positions, expanding class sizes, increased use of
technology, downloading of clerical tasks onto faculty, and the

shift to managerialism – all part of the corporatization of the
university. As the protagonist in David Lodge's most recent campus novel, *Deaf Sentence*, explains to a graduate student who com-
plains that her supervisor is never available: "He probably just
doesn't have enough time ... He's probably too busy attending
meetings, and preparing budgets, and making staff assessments,
and doing all the other things that professors have to do nowa-
days instead of thinking" (94). Reading *Deaf Sentence* provides a
constructive contrast to Lodge's earlier carnivalesque campus
fiction (*Changing Places* [1975], *Small World* [1984], and *Nice
Work* [1988]). In an article in the *Guardian*, Aida Edemariam
wonders why the satirical campus novel has been in decline
since the 1980s. "Maybe they were all elegies to an idea of the
campus," says Howard Jacobson: "Campuses have become trag-
ic places," he adds. In the heyday of the campus novel "you
could afford farce," explains A.S. Byatt, because universities
were intensely hopeful, whereas "now they're terrified and cow-
ering and underfinanced and overexamined and overbureau-
cratised" (qtd. in Edemariam 34).

The more we reflected on the links between our own experiences and the findings of the CAUT survey on occupational
stress, the more certain we became that individual professors'
well-being has far-reaching effects. We believe that our focus on
the professor is not entirely self-serving. It goes without saying
that stress is bad for the individual and has direct consequences
for society. The harmful effects of stress on our well-being,
health, and communities are widely documented and now generally acknowledged. What is less evident is that addressing individual professors' stress has political and educational ramifi-
cations. Although the original title for our book was *The Slow
Campus*, we changed it to *The Slow Professor* to highlight individual agency within the institutional context. Just as Slow Food re-
sists agribusiness by focusing on the small-scale producer, we
resist the corporate model's effacement of the role of the professor. In Bill Readings's analysis of the "posthistorical" (6) university, it is "the *administrator* rather than the professor" who is
the "central figure" in what is fast becoming a "transnational

bureaucratic corporation" (3). William Deresiewicz calls this "administrative elephantiasis" (par. 17). Similarly, Benjamin Ginsberg, in *The Fall of the Faculty: The Rise of the All-Administrative University and Why It Matters*, writes,

> Every year, hosts of administrators and staffers are added to college and university payrolls, even as schools claim to be battling budget crises that are forcing them to reduce the size of their full-time faculties. As a result, universities are filled with armies of functionaries – the vice presidents, associate vice presidents, assistant vice presidents, provosts, associate provosts, vice provosts, assistant provosts, deans, deanlets, deanlings, each commanding staffers and assistants – who, more and more, direct the operations of every school. (2)

Particularly striking is Ginsberg's analysis of universities' strategic plans which, rather than identifying unique strengths and future directions, are nearly identical. He concludes that the point is "not the plan but the process" (51): an "assertion of leadership" (49) and the erosion of the power of the faculty. It is the *appearance* of process that counts. Stefan Collini comments that the "fallacy of accountability" is "the belief that the process of reporting on an activity in the approved form provides some guarantee that something worthwhile has been properly done" (*What Are Universities For?* 108). The top-heavy university leads Frank Donoghue, in *The Last Professors: The Corporate University and the Fate of the Humanities*, to speak of the professor – defined as "autonomous, tenured, afforded the time to research and write as well as teach" (xi) – as nearing "extinction" (135). He speculates that soon we will be "practitioner-faculty," to use the term "coined by Apollo" Education Group, one of the largest for-profit educational service providers (97).

A surprising common thread in studies of the corporate university is an emphasis on change being in the hands of individual professors. It seems to be an effort to give us back a sense of agency within a potentially overpowering bureaucracy. While Jennifer Washburn in *University Inc.* does suggest policies for "safeguarding the universities' autonomy" (240), she says that equally if not more crucial is the "willingness" of individuals "to stand up and defend traditional academic values" (240). Readings explicitly avoids proposing policy changes, because, as he sees it, doing so serves only to exacerbate what is already a top-heavy institution. He is clear that he addresses his remarks to the professor rather than the administrator and "the scene of teaching" (the title of one of his chapters) rather than the provost's office. Our focus on the personal might seem solipsistic in the current climate, but we see individual practice as a site of resistance.

Moreover, faculty stress directly affects student learning. We know from experience that when we walk into a classroom breathless, rushed, and preoccupied, the class doesn't go well; we struggle to make connections with the material and our students. Hard data is beginning to emerge which confirms this. In a 2008 study reported in the *Journal of Educational Psychology* on "Teachers' Occupational Well-Being and the Quality of Instruction," researchers conclude that "a combination of high engagement ... with the capacity to emotionally distance oneself from work and cope with failure (resilience) is associated with both high levels of occupational well-being (low levels of exhaustion, high job satisfaction) and better instructional performance, and in turn leads to favorable student outcomes" (Klusmann et al. 702). In other words, professors' well-being is inextricably linked with students' learning. It seems ironic, however welcome, that students' stress is now fully recognized and addressed in the current climate, while their teachers are left to shift for themselves; the cynic may wonder whether this situation is symptomatic of the corporate university's emphasis on customer satisfaction. A 2014 article in the *Guardian Higher Education Network*, "Dark Thoughts: Why Mental Illness Is on the Rise in Academia," shows that little has changed in the seven years since the CAUT survey, confirming Claire Shaw and Lucy Ward's claim that there is a "culture of acceptance ... around mental health issues in academia" (par. 3). Workloads – particularly "demands for increased product and productivity" – have ballooned amidst an "uncaring academic environment" for faculty and graduate students (par. 13, 18). The notion of students as customers combined with greater reliance on technology has led to the increased blurring of work and life, with, for example, "demands such as 24-hour limit for responses to student queries" (par. 22).

When we look at studies of academic stress, we are struck by how many situations identified as sources of work stress are about lack of time. In the earliest study by Walter Gmelch, first published in 1984 and reproduced in 1993, the top ten self-reported stressors, in order of rank, are (1) "imposing excessively high self-expectations"; (2) "securing financial support for my research"; (3) "having insufficient time to keep abreast of current developments in my field"; (4) "receiving inadequate salary to meet financial needs"; (5) "preparing a manuscript for publication"; (6) "feeling that I have too heavy a workload, one that I cannot possibly finish during the normal working day"; (7) "having job demands which interfere with other personal activities (recreation, family, and other interests)"; (8) "believing that progress in my career is not what it should or could be"; (9) "being interrupted frequently by telephone calls and drop-in visitors"; (10) "attending meetings which take up too much time" (Gmelch 21–4). At least half of the categories (3, 6, 7, 9, 10) are explicitly about time poverty. In others (1, 5, 8), time is implied in measuring productivity: to feel that one's career is not progressing as it should means fearing it is not fast enough. Summarizing research findings on academic stress in 1987, Peter Seldin observes under the subheading "Too Many Tasks, Too Little Time" that this issue "tops the list of chronic work-related stress situations" (15). The time crunch has only worsened in the last two decades. More detailed and extensive studies were published in 2008 in a special issue on faculty time stress in the *Journal of Human Behavior in the Social Environment.* The various contributors to this volume identify additional sources of stress resulting from the rapidly changing university environment. These include "massive technological change" leading to "work overload"; "having jobs with no boundaries" (Miller et al. 3, 6, 12); "self-imposed expectations" which are "exceedingly high"

(Lindholm and Szelényi 20); and "environments of declining resources and increasing pressure to work as efficiently as possible" (Buckholdt and Miller 221). The CAUT report observes that perceptions of the once-desirable academic career "with high social standing," have changed considerably in the last twenty years. Commenting on previous studies in Australia and the UK, the CAUT team notes that common sources of stress – "workload, degree of task difficulty, and time pressure" – are "aggravated by restructuring, use of short-term contracts, external scrutiny and accountability, and major reductions in funding" (Catano et al. 7). The chief issue in the "Major Findings," is time: "Work-life balance was the most consistent stress-related measure predicting low job satisfaction and negative health symptoms" (Catano et al. 6). Lack of time, in other words, has serious consequences. As Mark C. Taylor puts it, "Speed Kills," and the casualties are many: "As acceleration accelerates, individuals, societies, economies, and even the environment approach meltdown" (par. 15).

While much has been written on the corporatization of universities, its effect on time begs further attention: corporatization has led to standardized learning and a sense of urgency. As Bill Readings argues in *The University in Ruins,* education now is "the passage from ignorance to enlightenment in a particular time span" (one which is as short and standardized as possible); "teaching is reduced" to "credit hours"; and "'Time to completion' is now presented as the universal criterion of quality and efficiency in education" (127, 128). Frank Donoghue argues that the "market categories of productivity, efficiency, and competitive achievement, not intelligence or erudition, already drive ... the academic world" (xvi). The values of productivity, efficiency, and competition have time as the common factor. Productivity is about getting a number of tasks done in a set unit of time; efficiency is about getting tasks done quickly; and competition, in part, is about marketing your achievements before someone else beats you to it. Corporatization, in short, has sped up the clock. Moreover, Stefan Collini, among others, has drawn attention to the damaging "no standing still" conception of "excellence" in the current academic ethos: "Standards must always be 'driven up'. Benchmarks exist to be surpassed" (*What Are Universities For?* 109, 18). It is extremely difficult to resist the universities' ever onward and upward mentality: "the 'excellent' must become 'yet more excellent' on pain of being exposed as complacent or backward-looking or something equally scandalous" (*What Are Universities For?* 109). Employing the example of a British university advertising for an administrator who would take the institution "beyond excellence," Collini points out that "the notion of 'continuous improvement' is conceptually incoherent" (*What Are Universities For?* 109–10).

The stakes are high. The opening sentence of Martha C. Nussbaum's manifesto *Not for Profit: Why Democracy Needs the Humanities* reads, "We are in the midst of a crisis of massive proportions and grave global significance" (1). James E. Côté and Anton L. Allahar's *Ivory Tower Blues* is subtitled *A University System in Crisis*. In Ginsberg's estimation, the "malignant growth" (203) of the all-administrative university is at an advanced stage: "some colleges and universities may be saved, but I fear that it may be too late at most schools" (39). Henry A. Giroux, in *The University in Chains: Confronting the Military-Industrial-Academic Complex*, provides yet another alarmist diagnosis: the "attacks" on higher education, he claims, "are much more widespread and, in my estimation, much more dangerous than the McCarthyite campaign several decades ago" (179). Frank Donoghue points out the ubiquity of the language of crisis. We also question the language of crisis but for reasons that differ from Donoghue, who "think[s] that professors of the humanities have already lost the power to rescue themselves" (xi).

We take a more optimistic approach. Ever since Martin Parker and David Jary proposed, in 1995, that higher education now takes place in the "McUniversity," notable for its "use of the consumer/student as a surrogate surveillance device" (326), there has been resistance to the pervasiveness of managerial power and corporate values. In 1997 Craig Prichard and Hugh Willmott, in "Just How Managed Is the McUniversity?," identified "some of the contradictions and struggles that make this broad shift unstable, partial and by no means inevitable" (287). The "impe-. rializing discourses and practices" of management "confront lo- cales in which there is often little enthusiasm for changing established traditions" on the part of those ostensibly managed (313). In 2001, Jim Barry, John Chandler, and Heather Clark argued that "the notion of resistance ... has been underplayed" (87), and their case study of two UK universities concluded that "managerialism is not fully embedded in university life":

> In the face of pressure from very senior levels in their universities and external sources, our academics and administrators *seek* to re- late to one another supportively as they *resist* the imposition of control in various ways. (Barry et al. 98, original emphasis)

And in 2012, Joëlle Fanghanel offers this potent reminder: "Academic roles ... are constructed and inhabited through navi- gating the tensions between structures, the communities in which practice takes place, and academics' own positions to- wards structures. Complexity and diversity stem as much from the structural conditions in which academics work (institutions, policy frameworks, academic conventions) as they do from the specific ways in which they respond as individuals to those condi- tions (their agentic positioning towards those, and their own beliefs about education and the academic endeavour)" (2). All of these researchers identify a space – in the words of Barry et al. – "Between the Ivory Tower and the Academic Assembly Line," arguing that those in "middle and junior levels ... are actively seeking to keep alive the craft of scholarship by mediating and moderating the harsher effects of the changes through support- ive or transformational styles of working" (87). Our chapter on collegiality explores what Frank Martela calls a "holding envi- ronment" (85), which offers respite from external managerial pressures and alleviates feelings of helplessness in the face of a putative "crisis."

Moreover, the discourse of crisis is part of the problem. While in their more recent *Lowering Higher Education: The Rise of Corpo- rate Universities and the Fall of Liberal Education*, Côté and Allahar qualify their definition of "crisis" as "a turning point ... rather than a situation of impending doom," they nevertheless maintain that the "university system has developed a set of problems that require some sort of decisive action *now*" (91). We do not deny that intervention is necessary, but we argue that the discourse of crisis creates a sense of urgency – act quickly before it is too late – which makes us feel even more powerless in the face of overwhelming odds. It is ironic that if the corporate model induces panic, so do the very books protesting corporate values. The discourse of crisis also inadvertently encourages passivity: if it's too late, why bother? We argue that approaching our professional practice from a perspective influenced by the Slow movement has the potential to disrupt the corporate ethos of speed. Slow living, as Parkins and Craig explain, "is not a simple matter of 'slowing down' but rather it is more fundamentally an issue of *agency*" (67). Slow Professors act with purpose, taking the time for deliberation, reflection, and dialogue, cultivating emotional and intellectual resilience, able, as Collini puts it, to hold our "nerve" (*What Are Universities For?* 85).

In response to the colleagues who have told us to wake up and get with the program or that they are simply too busy to slow down, we wish to emphasize that the Slow movement is "not a counter-cultural retreat from everyday life ... not a return to the past, the good old days ... neither is it a form of laziness, nor a slow-motion version of life" (Parkins and Craig ix). Rather, it is "a process whereby everyday life – in all its pace and complexity, *frisson* and routine – is approached with care and attention ... an attempt to live in the present in a meaningful, sustainable, thoughtful *and pleasurable* way" (Parkins and Craig ix). And we agree with Wendy Parkins and Geoffrey Craig that the Slow movement has the "potential" to not only "reinvigorate everyday life" (119) but also to repoliticize it (135). Indeed, one of the distinctive features of Slow Food is its combination of "Politics and Pleasure" – the subtitle of Geoff Andrews's *The Slow Food Story*. The focus on food is "rooted in [the] wider issues" of globalization and environmental concerns (17) while not losing sight of enjoyment. While Ginsberg describes his "proposed

therapeutic regimen" as "bitter medicine" (215), we want a cure
that not only will work but also feel good; we want to address
both the long term and the short term of one's daily life. In the
chapters that follow we will explore the ways in which the principles of Slow philosophy already mentioned, as well as the emphasis on conviviality and the local, are relevant to addressing faculty
stress and to transforming academic practice. As Jennifer A.
Lindholm and Katalin Szelényi emphasize, "significant numbers
of men and women faculty of all races and across all disciplines
and institutional types report that they experience extensive levels of work-related stress. Within this context, it is critical that we
... strive to develop habits of conducting our work and our lives
in ways that promote both our own and others' well-being" (36).

Our book is neither an empirical study along the lines of
James Côté and Anton Allahar nor a comprehensive exposé of
the corporate university. Bill Readings, Martha C. Nussbaum,
Stanley Aronowitz, and Benjamin Ginsberg, among others, have
offered brilliant analyses of the consequences and social implications of the corporatization of liberal education. Thoroughly
convinced by their arguments, we believe that what is needed
now is not another study diagnosing the problem. The contribution we hope to make combines politics with pleasure. What began simply as helping each other became a sustained examination
of academia. We see our book as uncovering the secret life of the
academic, revealing not only her pains but also her pleasures.
Writing this book provoked the anxiety of speaking what is habitually left unspoken, and we continually needed to remind
ourselves that the oscillation between private shame and the political landscape would prove fruitful. We came to recognize that
anxiety is the inevitable consequence of breaking taboos that
are not just current but have a long-standing history: the ideals
of mastery, self-sufficient individualism, and rationalism prop up
the "old" as well as the "new" university. In fact, patriarchal values opened the door to corporatization.

Perhaps we feel the threat to the university more keenly, situ-
ated as we are in the humanities. Ironically, our feelings of lack
of productivity and not measuring up have not led us until now

to "read" the institution; our self-blame has played into corporate values. As many have commented, there has been little protest from academics to the attack on the core principles of the university. It is not only that academics are "run off their feet" (Menzies and Newson, "Over-Extended Academic" par. 3) but also that the individualistic and meritocratic values of academic training inhibit collective awareness. While the humanities in particular have been vulnerable in the corporate university, they are paradigmatic of the non-instrumental intellectual enquiry which we need to protect across disciplines. It is precisely this critical thinking that is at the heart of the university as a public good rather than as "a merely sectional or self-interested cause on the part of current students and academics" (Collini, *What Are Universities For?* xi).

We envisioned this project, in part, as a self-help book for academics, and hope that the book is structured for reader ease. After the chapter "Time Management and Timelessness," which offers an overarching analysis of the temporalities that govern our work and how we might resist them, the rest of the chapters focus on the distinct components of academic work (teaching, research, and collegiality).

Corporatization has engendered pervasive time pressure (and stress). Chapter one begins by examining advice literature on time management targeted specifically at academics. We argue that texts promising to offer solutions to the overwhelmed academic do not deliver. Rather, they celebrate overwork and the culture of speed. Furthermore, the advice literature tends to misconceive the nature of scholarly work and the conditions it requires. This chapter focuses on the connections between time pressure and personal stress, and suggests ways of alleviating the crunch. It provides a foundation for the chapters that follow and which extend the analysis of the deleterious effects of the culture of speed on the individual to an explicitly political argument about its effects on intellectual work, social critique, and engaged citizenship.

In chapter two, "Pedagogy and Pleasure," Maggie makes the case for preserving the live classroom in the face of increasing pressure to go online precisely because teaching is not a matter of delivering information or even knowledge. Although thinking is inevitably embodied and contextual, academia tends to neglect the emotional and affective dimension to teaching and learning, along with the advantages of thinking in groups. It is well known that positive emotions facilitate learning, so it seems reasonable to suggest that they will also enhance teaching. It is neither frivolous nor incidental to ensure that we enjoy ourselves in the classroom: it may be crucial to creating an environment in which students can learn. The chapter explores various strategies and techniques to optimize the pleasure and reduce the stress of our teaching.

In chapter three, "Research and Understanding," Barbara interrogates the effects of corporatization on scholarship. We are all familiar with (and probably tired of) what Collini terms the "Edspeak buzzwords" (*What Are Universities For?* 78): our research is to be competitive, ground-breaking, cutting-edge, relatable, applicable, impactful, transferable, research cluster grant-winning, profit-generating, and easily packaged for media coverage (a photo, please!). A recent university billboard proudly announcing that the research conducted on its premises "cures deadly diseases" encapsulates this. These days, research into diseases that merely reduce an individual's quality of life are decidedly second-rate ... (and if you happen to be working on the novels of Proust, you rank even further down the list). Corporatization not only has prioritized certain areas of research above others but also has infiltrated the ways in which all of us, across the disciplines, conduct our research and the way we think about research. The push towards the easily quantifiable and marketable rushes us into "findings," and is at odds with the spirit of open inquiry and social critique. The chapter proposes a counter-discourse of Slow scholarship, understanding, and ethical engagement.

In chapter four, "Collegiality and Community," we address the loss of collegiality in the corporate university, identifying the possible causes and its demonstrated effects on our well-being and professional development. We contend that adding collegiality to teaching, research, and service only exacerbates the current chilly climate by further instrumentalizing us. Evaluating our ostensible commitment to collegiality turns us into measurable commodities not only to the administration but, worse, for each other. We suggest switching our attention to the neglected affective dimension of our work in order to create what Frank Martela calls "holding environments" (85) of mutual support and trust. Seeing collegiality in terms of solving emotional problems together may offer a more effective (and affective) intervention into the hyper-rational corporate context.

The conclusion, "Collaboration and Thinking Together," reflects on the process of co-authoring this project, and the ways in which it differed dramatically from single authorship. The contrast emerged within the parameters of the project itself when we decided to draft chapters two and three independently. Writing in the first person was much more difficult. Working together was one of the ways of putting Slow philosophy into practice, combining politics and pleasure.

Chapter One

Time Management and Timelessness

Creativity is the product of "wasted" time.

Albert Einstein, qtd. in Posen 172

In "Conflicting Time Perspectives in Academic Work," Oili-Helena Ylijoki and Hans Mäntylä observe, "It seems evident that whenever two or more academics happen to meet they complain about the lack of time" (56). A faculty survey conducted by MIT in 2001 made a surprising finding in a comparison between university faculty and CEOs. Seventy-eight percent of faculty reported that "no matter how hard they work, they can't get everything done" compared to 48% of CEOs, and 62% of faculty reported that they "feel physically or emotionally drained at the end of the day" compared to 55% of CEOs (MIT "Findings" 10). We were asked in a workshop whether any research had been done on personality types in higher education: Is it that perfectionists are attracted to university teaching and research? We believe that the question is somewhat misplaced: rather we should ask what it is about the university system that makes people feel unable to cope. It speaks volumes that Harry Lewis and Philip Hills, in *Time Management for Academics*, deem it necessary to state that "we have a *right to health*" and "We have a *right to a private life*, to a family life, to some waking time on personal projects (even to keep up with the mundane necessities of existence: getting ourselves housed, clothed and fed, paying bills, attending to basic maintenance); and so a right to limit our total working time in such a way as to allow for these activities" (109). The fact that we need to give ourselves permission to eat, bathe, and pay bills reflects our loss of balance in the current university climate. The time crunch is not just a personal issue. It is detrimental to intellectual work, interfering with our ability to think critically and creatively. Time management books promise us relief, but they often make us feel inadequate. We believe that it is not so much a matter of managing our time as it is of sustaining our focus in a culture that threatens it.

Academic work is by its nature never done; while flexibility of hours is one of the privileges of our work, it can easily translate into working all the time or feeling that one should. Mary Morris Heiberger and Julia Miller Vick note this paradox: "Despite their heavy workloads, academics have more freedom to structure their own time than practically anyone else in the economy. For some people, this is the great advantage of the career path; for others, it is a source of stress" (11). Furthermore, given the time and money required to get a PhD and its uncertain economic returns, it is clear that most of us pursue an academic career for idealistic, rather than pragmatic, reasons. And while believing in what one does is a key aspect of job satisfaction, idealism also can lead to overwork. The very idealism that drives intellectual and pedagogic endeavours is easily manipulated by the university which, like many other corporations, uses the rhetoric of family and community, "to solidify company cultures and inspire loyalty and commitment in an attempt to boost productivity" (Philipson 123). The irony is that the more committed we are to our vocation, the more likely it is that we will experience time stress and burnout.

While the characters in David Lodge's earlier campus novels had time on their hands – in *Changing Places*, Philip Swallow's visiting position at Euphoria State University is spent experimenting with sex, drugs, and rock and roll – today's professor scans the bookshelf or the Internet for the quick time fix. There is plenty of advice out there on time management for academics. Some of it, originating in the business sector, strikes one as

Machiavellian, such as that offered by Scribendi, an editing firm. One of their top ten time management techniques for academics is "use your grad students": "send the majority of undergrad complaints their way and have the grad students complete most of the marking. If they're going on to or are already in PhD studies, it's a good thing. You're doing them a favor. If they're not, well, it's part of being a grad student. Just make sure to treat them nicely – maybe buy a pizza during midterm marking or occasionally meet them at the pub and buy a round" (par. 4). Other tips in the service of saving time are "Keep a clock on your wall that only you can see" (Scribendi par. 2) and "stand up" (Scribendi par. 3) when students or colleagues drop by your office. Such strategies are echoed in texts such as Anastassia Ailamaki and Johannes Gehrke's "Time Management for New Faculty," which recommends that we *"Delegate as many tasks as possible to ... administrative assistants"*: "try to avoid making copies, finding flight schedules, ordering items over the Internet, and printing papers" (103). This curiously exploitative attitude seems to be an externalization of the pressure directed at ourselves: being driven, we drive others. These suggestions are blissfully ignorant of principles of unionized labour and the fact that administrative assistants and graduate students don't have unlimited time to devote to us either. In fact, professors are dealing with the exact opposite of delegation; for example, many clerical tasks (ordering desk copies, preparing cheque requisitions, photocopying, etc.) have been added to professors' to-do lists. Ailamaki and Gehrke also recommend having graduate students do some of our work when it comes to peer review of articles: "Give the paper to one of your students and schedule a meeting to discuss the paper within a couple of weeks. During this time, you also read the paper carefully. Then in a meeting with the student, you discuss the review, and the student writes a first draft that you can then review. This way we teach our students how to write good reviews, and at the same time there is a deadline by when the review will be well underway" (104–5). It seems that in the corporate university it's every academic for himself. The above strategies are symptomatic of the unrealistic work expectations in the current climate, leaving academics desperately grasping at strategies so that they can complete their "to-do" list.

If you are struggling to regain work-life balance, most academic time management literature will not leave you comforted. You may actually feel that you are not working hard enough. Gregory Colón Semenza's *Graduate Study for the Twenty-First Century* stipulates that "For the most part, an approximately ten-hour day is more than adequate for most academics, especially since we really can *work* for most of this time" as opposed to the general workforce which "waste[s] a tremendous amount of time commuting to and from work, chit-chatting at the water cooler, and lunching for a full hour" (48). His own exemplary regimen "finds me at my desk no later than 7:30 AM and gets me 'home' no earlier than 6:00 PM or so ... Of course, I will frequently need to work extra hours – when I receive student papers, have to meet an article deadline, or take an hour during the day to visit the doctor" (48). Under the subheading of "Eight Days a Week," he recommends his readers "be smart about which work you save for the weekends": "If on a Thursday I realize that I'll need to read two books and grade ten papers by Monday, I'll tackle the papers on Friday afternoon since I can more easily sneak in reading at various times and places over the weekend – in the living room while my wife reads her own book and my son naps, in the backseat on the way to Aunt Joanie's barbeque, or in the beach chair while I catch some rays. I can update attendance books while watching the Yankees. I can copy edit a manuscript while sitting at the park" (51). Philip C. Wankat, in *The Effective, Efficient Professor*, advises that "for most people, around 55 hours of work per week will get the most work done" (18), urging that even during the tenure probation period (which "is similar to wartime" [18]), it should "approach" that range (19) – which suggests more than 55 hours. He emphasizes that "family and personal life are important" (17), but when do we find time for them? We are struck by how much of time management advice seems to be contradictory; on the one hand, we are told that we need to exercise, eat well, pursue hobbies, and socialize so we can work at optimal levels, but the postulated hours of work preclude actually doing so. A 55-hour week looks something like this: 9:00 a.m. to 12 noon; 1:00 p.m. to 3:00 p.m.; 3:30 p.m. to 7:30 p.m., six days a week. We are confronted with a similarly relentless pace when Donald Hall, arguing that a research profile is possible even with a 4/4 teaching assignment when you "set ... realistic daily and weekly goals" (Hall and Lanser 221), suggests protecting Saturdays for research and deferring marking and class preparation to "twelve hours" on Sunday (222). Again, let's break this down: this means working 8:00 a.m. to noon, 1 to 6 in the afternoon, and 7 to 10 at night – on Sunday! Alec Mackenzie's *The Time Trap* includes among "Top Time Managers" the model of then chancellor of the University of Missouri, Kansas City, Dr Eleanor Brantley Schwartz, for inspiration, worth quoting in full:

> Time management is central in my life. In order for me to be productive with my jam-packed schedule, I need to plan the slots in which each necessary thing will get done and then see that it gets done within that slot.
>
> I have always had a busy life from the time when I was in school, held a full-time job, and was raising two children as a single parent. This could have been a high-stress situation, so I developed time management techniques out of sheer necessity. I would write from 4 A.M. until 6:45 A.M. when I would wake the children. We always did as much preparation as possible for going to work and going to school the night before. We tried to have everything we needed by the door and lunches prepared the night before and waiting in the refrigerator. Now I have household staff, but they, too, must be managed.
>
> I have always tried to do two things at once, when the tasks permit this. For example, once I got dinner started, I folded clothes as I kept the dinner preparation moving. Or I would write papers in my head, while cleaning up the kitchen and doing dishes. (211–12)

With some trepidation, we confess that these models of time management and productivity strike us as unrealistic and simply not sustainable over the long haul for most people. If, as Robert Boice says, we live in a culture that values "displays of busyness" (*First-Order Principles* 38), we propose a counterculture, a Slow culture, that values balance and that dares to be sceptical of the professions of productivity. To write at 4:00 a.m. means getting up around 3:30 a.m., which is the middle of the night. And if we do that consistently, what kind of energy will we have for the rest of the day's work and what will be the quality of our interactions with loved ones when we are consistently "doing two things at once"? A number of books, such as Dave Crenshaw's *The Myth of Multitasking* and Edward M. Hallowell's *CrazyBusy*, demonstrate that multitasking does not live up to its name. We are not doing two things at once – we are switching from task to task which not only makes us ineffective (as it takes time to refocus each time) but also makes us miss things. David Posen proposes "*single-tasking*" as "remedy": "do one thing at a time, sequentially, and with full attention" (164). Zadie Smith seems to agree: the acknowledgments for her novel *NW* open with "For creating the time ... Freedom©, Self-Control©" (295): programs that block Internet access. Academic culture celebrates overwork, but it is imperative that we question the value of busyness. We need to interrogate what we are modelling for each other and for our students. A recent issue of the *Queen's Alumni Review* includes an article by Julie Harmgardt, graduate and winner of the Arts and Science Undergraduate Society Scholarship. Harmgardt's InvisAbilities initiative, "an organization dedicated to promoting awareness, education, and support of young adults who are living with chronic, invisible illnesses such as arthritis, fibromyalgia, diabetes, lupus, and Crohn's disease" (8) is commendable and important, but what is disturbing is her description of the life she led as a student doing this work. While admitting that her treatment of adequate sleep as optional "doesn't promote wellness of body, mind, and spirit," "something's got to give in the rat-race" (8). Her "efforts to live each '25-hour' day to the fullest" required multitasking: "I would squeeze in fitness while catching up with a friend, take a book everywhere I went to fit in 10 extra minutes of my course readings, fold InvisAbilities brochures while skyping with my family, and attend large social gatherings so I could see lots of friends at one time" (9). We need to challenge the success stories of time management that promote multitasking and long hours. And we need to think critically about why time management is so strikingly uniform. These accounts of 9:00 a.m. to 7.30 p.m. six days a week (Wankat), or writing from 4:00 a.m. to 6.45 a.m. every morning (Schwartz), or scheduling every hour for the next several months (Hall) are curiously compelling. Is it that they justify our profession in our own minds as part of the labour force? Or that they promise we will finally get control? Or do they help us explain why we're not Michel Foucault (though Foucault apparently had a favourite ice-cream parlour opposite the library where he worked [theory.org])? If we allow ourselves to be impressed by Schwartz's work habits, we are getting sucked into what Hillary Rettig calls "perfectionist comparisons" which are "*always* invalid." This is because we will

> *always* come out on the losing end of any comparison – because the point of a perfectionist comparison is not to yield useful insight, but to serve as yet another club to bash yourself over the head with to try to coerce yourself into more productivity. (27)

One of us recalls running into a colleague by the waterfront one late August day and asking how his summer was going. "What summer?" he replied, "I've been writing eight hours a day." She felt terribly guilty that she had just been swimming with her daughter. It wasn't until she wrote this that she realized her colleague was out by the waterfront also, though presumably not enjoying it. As Rettig rightly points out, guilt and self-reproach do not make us more productive; they only create a "context fundamentally hostile to creativity" (32). We will discuss the conditions for creativity in more detail later, but for now Rettig offers some sane advice: "instead of measuring yourself against an impossible or exceptional productivity standard, measure yourself against a reasonable one while meanwhile working to uncover, and duplicate, the reasons for your occasionally higher productivity" (27).

Texts on time management are remarkably similar in their advice: keep a log to see where your time is "going," schedule every day, establish short-term and long-term goals, organize your workspace, and learn to say "no." While the dictum to plan, prioritize, and organize is not wrong, it tends to exacerbate our anxiety over time poverty by always measuring it. Dividing our time pie into ever smaller and precise segments is not a long-term solution. In this sense, time management is rather like the myriads of diets (indeed, some time management books explicitly make this comparison) which exhort us to keep a food diary, plan meals, set goals, and count the calories we take in and the ones we spend. Again, although this is not incorrect, it does not sufficiently take into account the reasons we may overeat in the first place and the systemic factors which have contributed to the "obesity epidemic." Similarly, like the dietary focus on the restriction of calories which produces deprivation (in turn, leading one to eat a family-size bag of chips and a pint of ice cream in a single sitting), time management books tend to engender deprivation, a sense of time poverty, with less-than-desirable results. Over and over again we are told that time is short. To capitalize on this precious resource, we are advised to schedule meetings for "less time than I think they're really going to take in the hope that it will make me and the other members more efficient" (Cuny 51) or, when preparing for travel, to "pack enough work in your carry-on for at least two hours longer than the flight is *supposed* to last" (Wankat 31). Ian Nelson urges teachers to fill every available time slot in their diary "as a powerful reminder of how little time you have. As long as you have some spaces in your diary it looks as though you have time in hand (23–4).

And then, of course, time is also money. Lewis and Hills write that we need to accustom ourselves, "both as individuals and as members of decision-making bodies, ... [to] treating our time and effort as a 'scarce resource' in the way that we treat money; as a resource that is strictly limited" (108). Yet, as Ylijoki and Mäntylä argue, the time pressures experienced by their interviewees result from the "management time" of the university in which "time is almost literally treated as a form of money that can be measured, counted and divided into units" (73), so that "The academics' everyday work has to be transformed into quantifiable measures and results irrespective of the internal rhythms of the work itself" (74). A pronounced example is "project researchers [who] keep a record of every half hour and document what they have been doing during that time. This is said to be done for the sake of invoicing so that researchers are able to demonstrate to the funding bodies how they have utilized their time, thus legitimizing their salaries" (61). This version of what it means to be accountable runs counter to how research unfolds in practice (9:00 a.m. to 9:30 a.m.: wrote a sentence; 9:30 a.m. to 10:00 a.m.: decided to delete same sentence; ordered a book on interlibrary loan; etc.).

Endless opportunities for humour aside, such record-keeping is hopelessly impractical for research and reading (e.g., how many pages we read in an hour will vary widely on what we're reading and for what purpose). Donald E. Hall's *The Academic Self: An Owner's Manual* emphasizes "manag[ing] ... time wisely" (44) to the point of scheduling each month of academic work ahead of time "hour by hour" (49). Given that "time is subdividable, regular, and predictable," "it is imperative that we know from the outset how many days, even hours, we can devote to a specific process – research, pedagogical, or communal – in the coming weeks, months, or even a year or more" (48). Is academic time really as "subdividable, regular, and predictable" (48) as Hall posits? Our classes are, but many other parts of our work simply are not. There are rhythms to the teaching term, but we cannot anticipate the number of students who will approach us for letters of reference, the number of scholarship applications which will arrive for us to assess and rank, the number of plagiarism cases requiring us to take action, and so on, and thus it is impossible to schedule each hour of a working day a month ahead.

The problem with even the most well-intentioned time management plans such as Hall's is that they plug us in to the wrong kind of time, scheduled time, which tends to exacerbate the feelings of fragmentation that result from juggling teaching, research, administration, self-reporting, student emails, etc. The word "fragmentation" crops up repeatedly in Ylijoki and Mäntylä's interviews of Finnish academics. Working days have "become very long and fragmented," and "fragmentation of time and energy is perceived by academics as seriously undermining their work satisfaction and their productivity" (56). The sense that there is never enough time produces panic, a feverish sense of being always behind. As Ellen Ostrow observes, "So often, when you work under pressure, there's an ongoing conversation inside your head. It usually includes thoughts about what you 'should' be doing, 'what if' scenarios, and thoughts about how you can scramble to get everything done" (par. 19). Meghan Telpner, in her critique of conventional dietary regimens, proposes that what we really need is an "Undiet" – the title of her book. Similarly we propose we need not time management, but timelessness.

We believe that the problems of time stress will not be solved with better work habits (and if you doubt this, reader, please remember that you managed to complete graduate school or are in the process of doing so). Time management does not take into full account the changes to the university system: rather, it focuses on the individual, often in a punitive manner (my habits need to be pushed into shape). The real time issues are the increasing workloads, the sped-up pace, and the instrumentalism that pervades the corporate university. The fact that requests for information from some deans and directors to faculty now stipulate "end of business Friday" or "COB (close of business)" as a deadline makes clear that we increasingly are caught between two temporalities: corporate time and the time conducive for academic work. What has been called "timeless time" as "the internally motivated use of time in which clock time loses its significance," has become largely an object of wishful thinking (62). Ylijoki and Mäntylä's survey of fifty-two Finnish academics – in which no questions were directly asked about temporal aspects of their work – revealed that all regarded timeless time as a "luxury," the subject either of nostalgia or "a wish, a plan and an aim," rather than a reality (63, 64). These academics also reported that insufficient time made them feel "powerless and stressed"

(56). The link between time pressure and feelings of powerlessness needs to be further investigated, particularly because both are related to the shift of power into the hands of university administrators whose concern with economics results in pressure for everything to be done efficiently. Ylijoki and Mäntylä observe that "true research takes – and must be allowed to take – all the time it needs" (63), a claim which seems extraordinarily radical in the current climate. This is the rallying call of the Slow Science Academy, whose manifesto insists,

unless you need publication

> We do need time to think. We do need time to digest. We do need time to misunderstand each other, especially when fostering lost dialogue between humanities and natural sciences. We cannot continuously tell you what our science means; what it will be good for; because we simply don't know yet. Science needs time.
> – *Bear with us, while we think.* (slow-science.org)

As Bodil Jönsson writes, "surely we know that intellectual work, such as research (the creation of new knowledge) and learning (the creation of new knowledge within oneself), must be measured in a way totally different from the way we measure the work of industrialization" (95) and she concludes that "what we need is thinkology rather than technology" (96). This chapter, in part, is our attempt at "thinkology."

In order to think critically and creatively, or even just to be able to think straight, we need, as Ylijoki and Mäntylä point out, "timeless time" (62). Timelessness is defined by Charalampos Mainemelis as "the experience of transcending time and one's self by becoming immersed in a captivating present-moment activity or event" (548). Research shows that periods of escape from time are actually essential to deep thought, creativity, and problem solving. Mihaly Csikszentmihalyi discovered after extensive research into the lives of people across a range of occupations and ethnicities that the more a person experiences "flow," the happier he or she will be. Csikszentmihalyi goes so far as to claim that "flow" – an "optimal state of inner experience ... in which there is *order in consciousness*," makes us better people:

This happens when psychic energy – or attention – is invested in realistic goals, and when skills match the opportunities for action. The pursuit of a goal brings order in awareness because a person must concentrate attention on the task at hand and momentarily forget everything else. These periods of struggling to overcome challenges are what people find to be the most enjoyable time of their lives ... A person who has achieved control over psychic energy and has invested it in consciously chosen goals cannot help but grow into a more complex being. By stretching skills, by reaching toward higher challenges, such a person becomes an increasingly extraordinary individual. (6)

This experience of "flow" is so elusive that it can only be captured retroactively, once it's all over. Frustratingly, it is defined by Mainemelis in a tautology:

Timelessness is the experience of transcending time and one's self by becoming immersed in a captivating present-moment activity or event. Scholars and poets have suggested over the years that the timeless intensity of the present moment is a gateway to creativity and joy. (548)

When we experience timelessness, we are creative, and creativity is experienced as timelessness.

We cannot order "flow" online – in fact we shall see that is the last place where we will find it – but we can order the conditions, the timeless time that fosters creativity, original thinking, and, as a bonus apparently, joy. Recognizing that the availability of timeless time paradoxically increases the productivity of organizations, Mainemelis examined the conditions that either foster or impede "highly focused, imaginative, and quality work" (559), which is "defined as the work output of an individual that is novel, original, and useful" (549). Not surprisingly, he found that "certain task, person, and work environment factors" all contribute to "the likelihood that one will be creative at work" (553). The first two conditions are largely taken care of in the university setting. Academics are usually highly intrinsically motivated by their work; they believe they have worthwhile goals and the capacities to pursue them; they know that "creativity ... requires passion, persistence, and perseverance," and they expect to apply themselves "over long periods of time in generating and elaborating upon creative ideas" (560). It seems that academics are exemplary candidates for states of flow. But personal motivation is not enough. Environmental factors facilitate or interfere with creative thinking. The major obstacle to creative and original thinking, Mainemelis found, is the stress of having too much to do:

> Extreme workload pressures in particular, in the form of extreme time pressures and unrealistic expectations for productivity ... make it virtually impossible for individuals to become engrossed in the task at hand and to experience timelessness. (559)

We need, then, to protect a time and a place for timeless time, and to remind ourselves continually that this is not self-indulgent but rather crucial to intellectual work. If we don't find timeless time, there is evidence that not only our work but also our brains will suffer.

Timelessness is clearly desirable not only for our work but also for our professional and personal satisfaction. But it is pushed to the margins by more immediate and pressing demands. Research days ideally are spent writing and poking in the library, but instead we catch up with emails and record-keeping while trying to master the latest technological application because we have been told, in an email from above, that the university has purchased this system and it is now in use (and then there are those of us who admit that they spent yet another research day burnt out and unproductive). As Mainemelis puts it, citing Csikszentmihalyi and others: "A normal state of consciousness is characterized by disharmony, because a myriad of different stimuli compete for limited attention resources." What we need instead is "engrossment," which "mobilizes one's entire attention resources and physical energy toward only one stimulus, which is the present-moment activity" (556). There is, observes Maura

Thomas, "an abundance of noise in our lives" (24). David Shenk, reflecting on his book *Data Smog* ten years later, observes, "The problem seems to be that we're wired to turn our attention to commotion" (Shenk "E Decade" par. 10). So, how do we turn down the commotion and why should we?

1. We need to get off line. Tom Chatfield, in *How to Thrive in the Digital Age*, recognizes that for the first time in history "many people's daily default is to be 'wired' into at least one personalized form of media" (30). We now have, he says, two "fundamentally different ways of being in the world: our wired and unwired states," and we need to ask "which aspects of a task, and of living, are best served by each" (31). Shenk, among others, tells us that research shows that "it takes an *experienced* computer user an average of 15 minutes to return to 'serious mental tasks' after answering email or instant messages" (Shenk "E Decade" par. 4). If we are continually interrupted virtually, we cannot help but be fragmented. If we keep checking messages, we suffer from what Thomas calls "self-induced ADD" (9). The Internet, as Nicholas Carr has shown, is actually changing our brains:

> Given our brain's plasticity, we know that our online habits continue to reverberate in the workings of our synapses when we're not online. We can assume that the neural circuits devoted to scanning, skimming, and multitasking are expanding and strengthening, while those used for reading and thinking deeply, with sustained concentration, are weakening or eroding. (141)

The main problem with multitasking is summed up memorably by Michael Merzenich in an interview: "We are 'training our brains to pay attention to the crap.' The consequences for our intellectual lives may prove 'deadly'" (qtd. in Carr 142).

2. We need to do less. Rettig's wonderful book *The Seven Secrets of the Prolific* says:

> Time management is not about jamming as much as possible *into* your schedule, but eliminating as much as possible *from* your

schedule so that you have time to get the important stuff done to a high degree of quality and with as little stress as possible. (80)

We will probably need to brace ourselves for criticism: "That's why I tell people that if, after you start managing your time, people start complaining, congratulations! It means you're doing it right" (Rettig 77). David Posen, in *Is Work Killing You?*, points out that doing less actually achieves more. We all have a maximum capacity for productive work and sustained thinking, and once the peak is passed we are simply putting in time, which is pointless (since the work will not be of high quality) (87–92). Posen's research finds that "working long hours is often inefficient, and that, when people have too much stress, they're less productive" (67). He cites many reasons for organizations' resistance to his proposals for reducing working hours and workplace stress, but the one that stands out is what he calls "Peer pressure and corporate culture": "Overwork is seen as strength, and work-life balance is viewed as weakness or self-indulgence" (71). Along with doing less, then, it seems we need to keep Posen's and Rettig's books on our desks for needed affirmation.

3. We need regular sessions of timeless time. As Thomas puts it succinctly, "The less you allow yourself the opportunity to focus the less focused you will be" (25).

These sessions require:

a) a transition, "a personal rite of passage … to focus attention, reduce anxiety, create a playful atmosphere, and so forth" (Mainemelis 555).

b) an acknowledgment that the task will take longer than you planned. Try expecting it to take twice as long. And keep in mind "*setup time*": "The time it takes to put things in order, to arrange things so that you can start on a specific task" (Jönsson 34). And keep in mind that the first time you do anything it takes more time.

c) playfulness. Creativity involves and even demands a kind of playfulness. Chatfield observes that "The kind of thoughts that can emerge in 'empty' time in our lives … are impossible to reproduce either through dedicated digital planning or carefully arranged offline sessions. They are moments that steal up on us, most often, when *life is not segmented down to the minute*" (49, emphasis added).

d) silencing the "inner bully" (as Rettig [21] calls it). We need to silence the critics in our own heads:

> What usually kills or blocks one's creativity is lack of courage to explore novel or countercultural ideas, paralyzing anxiety about one's performance, and premature rejection of one's insights as inadequate or not worthy of further elaboration. (Mainemelis 559)

e) turning off the voices of the mythical tax-paying public (again in our own heads). Collini writes that "One of the most dispiriting features of the current climate of discussion is the background implication ... that universities are something of a luxury ... and that many academics are little better than middle-class welfare-scroungers, indulging their hobbies at public expense" (Collini *What Are Universities For?* 197–8).

4. We need <u>time to do nothing</u>, or what Posen calls "timeouts." The cerebralism of professorial identity may make us bristle at this, but we should remember that "our brains, like our bodies, need periodic rest. The brain is like a muscle. It gets tired. We need recovery time, downtime, and decompression time" (Posen 166). Many of us understand "decompression" as letting ourselves collapse at the end of the day or taking that much-needed vacation once a year. But we need more than that. The "timeouts" that this medical doctor prescribes are "pauses" in our workdays in order to be kind to ourselves (which has the ripple effect of kindness to those around us), as well as to protect and, in fact, enhance the quality of our work.

5. We need to change the way we talk about time all the time. Jönsson, in *Unwinding the Clock*, suggests that to change one's relationship to time, "you have to start getting used to thoughts about time other than such depressing statements as 'I just don't have enough time!,' 'There's no time!,' or 'I don't know how

I'm going to find the time'" (viii). Given that no day will ever have more than twenty-four hours, it is more useful to change our perception of the passing of time. As she puts it, "Plenty-of-time joy is no more wrong than the not-enough-time nightmare" (48). Again, we probably need to brace ourselves for pushback: "this sort of reasoning provokes other people. Both friends and strangers have demonstrated this by their questions, which are usually mixed with fear" (Jönsson 10).

This chapter has focused on the detrimental effects of time poverty on our well-being and the quality of our work, but time poverty is also political as we will explore in detail in the following chapters. The temporality of the corporate university does more, than contribute to personal stress (which is bad enough). It also undermines the democratic potential of the university, which is to encourage people "to think, to engage knowledge critically, to make judgements, to assume responsibility for what it means to know something, and to understand the consequences of such knowledge for the world at large" (Giroux "Attack on Higher Education" par. 3).

Chapter Two

Pedagogy and Pleasure

If we ask academics to hold students in a space of vulnerability and uncertainty in which they can embrace their own beings, it is necessary that we create the kind of environment where academics can explore their own vulnerability and uncertainty.

Blackie et al. 643

Slow teaching does not mean – contrary to the many jokes that come our way – s-p-e-a-k-i-n-g- v-e-r-y- s-l-o-w-l-y, nor does it entail doing less or expecting less from our students (desirable as these things may be). It is, however, related to time. Paradoxically, during a "Slow" class, time would fly by, and we would all – teachers and students – be surprised that it was over so soon. All of us want students who are enthusiastic about the material and appreciative of our efforts to make it clear. All students want teachers who are enthusiastic about the material and appreciate their efforts to comprehend it. We all want to leave the class energized. Last year Barbara and I were both fortunate enough to enjoy courses in which we eagerly anticipated the conversations with and among our students. Did this happen through sheer luck? Was it because (as we tended to assume) we had exceptionally keen and kindly students? What is the difference between an exhausting and an uplifting class? We realized that we were both teaching subject matter that we really cared about and that could, and did, change the way people think; both courses were a joy to teach. We were, to our surprise, engaging and even charismatic teachers (student evaluations indicated this), though we are not always so; in fact, one of us was teaching an unusually quiet and reticent class during the same term. We realized that our enjoyment was not merely a fortuitous by-product of the successful courses but rather was key. It seems obvious that when one teaches well, one enjoys it, but perhaps the reverse is actually more accurate: that when one enjoys teaching, one does it well. The current emphasis on "evidence-based practices" and "processes to measure impact" in teaching and learning entirely overlooks pleasure (Queen's Teaching and Learning Action Plan, 2014, 7); yet it may be the case that pleasure – experienced by the instructor and the students – is the most important predictor of "learning outcomes."

Pleasure is, as the Slow Food movement has made clear, inimical to the corporate world. While other radical political movements, as Geoff Andrews points out, neglected or even eschewed pleasure, Slow Food is "Politics in Search of Pleasure" (3). In a world which, in George Ritzer's words, is increasingly homogenized, "in which virtually anywhere one turns one finds very familiar forms of nothing," we need, as he puts it, "something" which is "locally conceived and rich in distinctive context" (Ritzer qtd. in Andrews 36). Our search for the distinctive pleasures of teaching and learning will take up Amanda Burrell and Michael Coe's challenge that "before 'live' lectures are abandoned in favour of remote class streaming, it is timely to examine what happens in a 'live' lecture when academics and students occupy the same space at the same time"("Be Quiet and Stand Still" 3170). The obvious difference between face-to-face and remote learning is the proximity of bodies and the transmission of emotions that inevitably follows. We focus here on live classes and on the politics of pleasure because both are obstructionist in the corporate university; and, as Ruth Barcan points out in *Academic Life and Labour in the New University*, "We have more control in the classroom than in macropolitics" (15). There are, Mary O'Reilley observes rather wryly, "some interesting studies on the relationship between stress and cynicism" in teaching; she asks: "but is there any way we can interrupt this hardening process and keep ourselves alive in the classroom?" (69). We believe that we can combat stress and cynicism – while keeping ourselves alive – by promoting a pedagogy of pleasure. Such a notion has the additional attraction of being antithetical to corporate values.

Intelligence: contextual and embodied

In light of the corporate university's penchant for everything quantifiable, one might expect to find widespread acceptance of a fixed and measurable "intelligence quotient," or IQ. On the contrary, the last decades have seen growing awareness that intelligence is embodied and therefore is dependent on context and emotions. David Brooks explains in "The Waning of I.Q." that investigations of the brain show that "far from being a cold engine for processing information, neural connections are shaped by emotion" (par. 8). Annie Murphy Paul summarizes research showing that the concept of a fixed and measurable IQ is an outdated myth. Instead, intelligence depends on circumstances: "Situational intelligence ... is the only kind of intelligence there is – because we are always doing our thinking in a particular situation, with a particular brain in a particular body" (par. 6). Learning does not and cannot take place in some transcendent brain. Antonio Damasio shows that even if it were possible to maintain a disembodied brain, that brain would not be able to think: "I am not saying that the mind is in the body. I am saying that the body contributes more than life support and modulatory effects to the brain. It contributes a *content* that is part and parcel of the workings of the normal mind" (226). One of Damasio's patients, whose damaged frontal cortex deprived him of emotions, was unable to make a simple decision: without emotion he could not think (45, 49). Academia's tendency to conceive the body as life support for the brain has had deleterious effects on our teaching (not to mention our lives). Renate Caine and Geoffrey Caine have successfully put into practice a pedagogy in schools based on the premise that "the body and brain so interpenetrate each other that at some level they need to be treated as a single system" (90). Our experiences convince Barbara and me that our own and our students' intelligence depends on the context and is particularly susceptible to the emotions generated by the group. In other words, it is not an illusion that when class goes well, we all think better; recent research agrees that we actually *are* all more clever (Paul).

Recognizing our own and our students' embodiment shifts the emphasis of our pedagogy. Examining student evaluations demonstrates the pervasiveness of emotions in the classroom. Words such as "inspiring," "stimulating," "engaging and thought-provoking" all express affect, so that "thinking and caring" about a topic – as one student put it – are frequently linked in a single phrase. Students, it seems, make no distinction between how they felt in a course and how they thought; their emotions – whether positive or negative – were integral to how they learned. Barbara L. Fredrickson's extensive research on the psychology of group dynamics has prompted her to formulate the "broaden and build" theory of positive emotions. Negative emotions were of evolutionary benefit to human beings, she surmises, because they prompted the quick and decisive action necessary to escape danger; positive emotions, on the other hand, resulted in what we could call higher-order activities. Previous analyses suggest that: "Joy, for instance, broadens by creating the urge to play, push the limits, and be creative ... Interest, a phenomenologically distinct positive emotion, broadens by creating the urge to explore, take in new information and experiences, and expand the self in the process" (220). Fredrickson's own experiments confirm that positive emotions increase our range of psychological, intellectual, and physical responses, or our "thought-action repertoires" (219). Moreover, positive emotions also make us psychologically resilient in the long term by undoing the damage done by negative emotions: "to the extent that positive emotions broaden the scopes of attention and cognition, enabling flexible and creative thinking, they should also augment people's enduring coping resources" and "enhance people's subsequent emotional well-being" (223). This is an impressive list of the immediate and lasting benefits of positive emotions. Who would not want creative, intellectually expansive, and resilient students?

Live lectures and affect

A 2004 "manifesto" on "affective learning" by ten experts at MIT Media Lab acknowledges that "affective functions and cognitive ones are inextricably integrated with one another" (Picard et al. 253) to such an extent that "a slight positive mood does not just make you feel a little better but also induces a different kind of thinking, characterised by a tendency toward greater creativity and flexibility in problem solving, as well as more efficiency and thoroughness in decision making" (254). The computer scientists at MIT quote M.R. Lepper and R.W. Chabay's point that "expert human tutors ... devote at least as much time and attention to the achievement of affective and emotional goals in tutoring" as they do to the "cognitive and informational" goals that are typical of computer learning (255). They aspire to develop new technologies that have "emotional intelligence" which can "recognise and respond to affect" (256). Artificial "EQ," as it is known, comprises abilities to recognize facial actions, vocal expressions, body movements, and skin temperature. The Galvactivator, for example, is a "skin-conductivity sensing glove" which can measure psychological arousal linked to a glowing LED which allows students to see the degree of their own engagement in a task (it was brighter when they were "discussing ideas" than "when they were lectured to") (257). A "physically animated computer" is being developed that will "move in subtly expressive ways in response to its user" (258). The device is inspired by "natural human-human interaction – when people work together, they move in reciprocal ways, such as shifting posture at conversational boundaries and leaning forward when interested" (258). In these technologies the emphasis is on detecting patterns of behaviour – through observation – and deducing the user's affective state: "The latter is what is termed 'emotion recognition' even though it does not really see what you are feeling, but only a pattern of measurable external changes associated with feelings" (256).

These attempts to replicate the affective conditions of human exchange seem to be missing the point: their emphasis on what is observable serves to reinforce the isolation they attempt to overcome. Teresa Brennan's *The Transmission of Affect* shows that we don't necessarily *see* what someone is feeling: we are more likely to *smell* it. Brennan argues convincingly that emotions are conveyed through pheromones (we've long accepted this about sexual attraction), so that affect is "literally in the air" and flows from person to person through olfaction. Perhaps the media lab should be working on a scratch-and-sniff delivery. The airborne chemicals that we take in actually alter our mood through our blood: "environment ... changes human endocrinology, not the other way around" (73). Science has neglected this olfactory means of transmitting emotion because it challenges Western beliefs that we are separate and bounded individuals whose emotions are contained in our own skins:

> The idea of self-containment is tied to the belief that cognition, more than emotion, determines agency, and it is not surprising that as the one (self-containment) comes to dominate in the history of ideas, so does the other (cognition). (62–3)

Our emphasis on cognition in the West, then, results from our individualistic philosophies.

Although Brennan does not address issues of pedagogy, her new paradigm for the transmission of affect has significant implications for distance and blended learning. The emphasis on sight in learning technologies reinforces a mind/body split along with a subject/object dichotomy (ironically, self-monitoring devices would make the learner into her own object). Because "knowledge ... gleaned by smell or touch or sound, does not always, or even habitually, penetrate the modern consciousness," says Brennan, it is overlooked (23); but it is also ignored because it undermines our cherished individualism: "The name or the concept of the transmission of affect does not sit well with an emphasis on individualism, on sight, and cognition" (18). In other words, much more happens in a live classroom than an exchange of ideas or even of observable patterns of emotional responses. If learning were purely or even predominantly cognitive, then computers would be adequate and there would be no point in gathering people together in a room. But affects are

social, "are there first, before we are" (65). The affective environment influences the nature of cognition: "affects may, at least in
some instances, find thoughts that suit them, not the other way
around" (7).

Emotions, Brennan explains, are transitory, but affect is the
lingering and pervasive residue of emotions. This suggests that
though it is important to maintain positive feelings in ourselves
and our students (as I write this it seems self-evident), we do not
need to maintain a constant "high." Colin Beard et al. discovered that by second year, university students "refer to pedagogic hardship as pleasurable"; they report the satisfaction of
"working hard," "being absorbed in work," and getting through
a challenging situation. Thus "complex blends of negative and
positive" emotions surface (637). Beard at al., citing Barnett,
find that in contrast to ephemeral pleasure, "'enduring ecstasy'
is experienced as joy and fulfilment when a student finally un-
derstands a difficult concept as potentially transformational"
(632). What motivates students to persist with difficulties are the
positive emotions arising from "affiliation" or belonging. Whereas "the positive emotions of drive/achievement give a 'high'
(opiates/ endorphins) ... affiliation has a positive calming effect (dopamine)" (631). We are sustained by "the sense of *belonging* within an academic community" (638).

In "The Ripple Effect: Emotional Contagion and Its Influence
on Group Behavior," Sigal Barsade describes experiments showing that group emotions do indeed exist and that they "can influence work outcomes" (645). Barsade's research confirms "that
people do not live on emotional islands but, rather, that group
members experience moods at work, these moods ripple out
and, in the process, influence not only other group members'
emotions but their group dynamics and individual cognitions,
attitudes, and behaviors as well" (670). "The development of
group emotion" is what distinguishes a community from "merely a collection of individuals" (644). Brennan's work on the social nature of affect inadvertently demonstrates the benefits of
'live' classes: "Collectivities may have more – rather than less –
intelligence, deductive speed, and inventiveness than the individuals within them" (Brennan 62). Students and teachers think

more effectively in the context of a community – as opposed to a collection of separate individuals – and while experiencing positive emotions. It hardly needs repeating that the courses which are a joy to teach are those in which we feel most connected to others.

Enjoying teaching

Enjoying our teaching will not only benefit our students but may actually combat the negative effects of the current academic climate. Fredrickson has shown that positive emotions loosen the hold on our psyches of negative ones: "Two distinct types of positive emotions – mild joy and contentment – share the ability to undo the lingering cardiovascular aftereffects of negative emotions" (222). We do not need to skip singing to class: "mild joy and contentment" are enough. Enjoyment is not superficial, not a matter of having fun – something which the scholar views with horror – but rather a matter of finding "positive meaning" in "ordinary events" and even "within adversity." Furthermore, positive emotions "increase the likelihood of finding positive meaning in subsequent events" (223).

It may not come as a surprise, however, that we need to work at having positive emotions. Rick Hanson explains that "the brain evolved a built-in *negativity bias* ... always on the lookout for potential dangers or losses" (20). The university classroom seems ripe for negative emotions: we may be anxious about our performance, and our students are likely anxious about theirs; above all academia is traditionally considered serious business. Whatever else we do, we need first, as O'Reilley memorably puts it, to stop abusing ourselves with overwork: "it doesn't help students ... learn, it ruins our health and causes us to have colourful breakdowns – but the most important reason is that it ultimately makes us hate students" (50).

My aim in the remainder of the chapter is to put teaching in slow motion for a moment in the hope that paying attention to how we feel will reduce anxiety (the brain's negativity bias) and increase our pleasure in the task (and maybe our overall happiness). I have chosen verbs – frequently gerunds – deliberately, because they help to capture the embodied emotions. What follows are my reflections combined with advice I have found helpful. None of it is surprising; in fact it may well strike you as obvious; obvious as it is, it is usually forgotten.

1. Entering class

Although I always leave time to gear up for class, doing so usually involves anxiously looking at my notes or second-guessing my PowerPoint slides. Unlike actors or athletes, professors do not prepare psychologically for class – it is even hard to imagine how we would. We rush from office hours or a meeting, arms full of books or papers, hoisting our laptop and hoping we've got the memory key. My most stressful moments are waiting for the previous teacher to unhook his technology and finish talking to his students; it doesn't help my state of mind that I resort to the hope that looks really can kill. Being conscious of a transition to class has vastly improved my state of mind.

A) BEING NERVOUS

I am a nervous teacher, but I've learned to accept it. The research I've done for workshops on what I called "The Fear of Teaching" finally enabled me, as Larry Danson puts it, "to re-evaluate my own feelings and interpret nervousness as eagerness" (qtd. in Showalter 17). Discovering that many great teachers experience "stage fright" was remarkably consoling; it was, surprisingly, even more reassuring to learn Parker J. Palmer's view that being a professor may be more nerve-wracking than being a celebrity:

> A good teacher must stand where personal and public meet, dealing with the thundering flow of traffic ... As we try to connect ourselves and our subjects with our students, we make ourselves, as well as our subjects, vulnerable to indifference, judgement, ridicule. (17)

Yet Palmer wrote this in 1998 before the roar in "traffic" had been increased by technology. Much of my nervousness originates in myths about the teacher's role inherited from past generations that I still carry around with me. Once I realized that authority, control, and encyclopedic knowledge could distance my students, I began to enjoy myself.

But I still need to deal with the physiological consequences: being aware of my dry mouth seems to set my heart beating faster. Sucking one of those tiny candies helps: I consumed nearly a whole box before a 400-strong plenary that I gave a few years ago and had to begin by telling the audience that I wasn't knocking back drugs. Thinking "Oh no! I'm so nervous!" causes the panic to spiral, whereas thinking "Oh, I'm nervous again – but that's OK," reduces the "fight or flight" reaction. I have tried singing on the way to class. The simplest advice I had was from my mum, in an entirely different context. Fed up with my phone calls home about my errant love-life, Mum said, "Try thinking about yourself a little less, dear." Although I was taken aback at the time, it has had countless effects on the way I teach. My mum's advice shifted the focus of attention away from my fears and onto what my students need.

B) PAUSING

A conscious transition to class has been shown to improve our teaching. Amanda Burrell, Michael Coe, and Shaun Cheah have developed successful workshops in Australia in which teachers adopt the simple strategy of beginning lectures by occupying the space, as actors do, with silence and stillness. The opening pause improves the teacher's confidence and delivery, the atmosphere in the room, and the students' attention. Burrell and Coe point out that "holding the space" signals confidence, authority, and having something worth hearing (3170). One participant in their workshops reflected that learning stillness and silence not only increased his confidence, but also enabled him to "foster a sense of connection with the students ... making them feel welcome and supported." He concluded that this "sense of confidence in communicating verbally and non-verbally ... really stems from the energy shown and the spontaneity of delivery, with the notion that teaching will be enjoyable" (Burrell, Coe, and Cheah 3245). Non-verbal communication has been shown to be more immediate than verbal; Barsade calls this "primitive emotional contagion": a "very fast process of automatic, continuous, synchronous nonverbal mimicry and feedback" (647). The students who unconsciously mimic our behaviour actually "experience the emotion itself ... through the physiological feedback from their muscular, visceral, and glandular responses" (648). Brennan would disagree with Barsade's assumption that the positive affect is transferred through mimicry, but she would certainly confirm Burrell et al.'s intuition that the atmosphere in the room happens as we enter and before we open our mouths to speak. Furthermore, the teacher's body language influences her own emotions: I always advised my graduate-student teachers to pretend to be someone who is confident. Then I discovered Amy Cuddy's experiments in body language and brain chemistry: she found that assuming an assertive pose just before an interview actually does make us more assertive.

c) BREATHING

Being aware of our breathing as we begin class can similarly calm us and our students. Joshua Searle-White and Dan Crozier plumb the subtler depths of communication when they suggest that our breathing mirrors our relationship with our students: "Are we willing to take the students and the classroom situation in and let them inform what we are then going to offer?" (4) We habitually breathe shallowly, they maintain, especially when sitting at the computer; yet shallow breathing in the classroom signals anxiety to our students: "Holding our breath as a student asks a question, for example, will make it physically more difficult to respond to the question because we will need to exhale first and rebalance our breathing before we can speak" (4–5). Breathing easily, on the other hand, "signals relaxation and can convey confidence and ease, and it may even make it easier for the students to concentrate on the class material" (5). Searle-White and Crozier focus on our own embodiment with the goal of creating "possibilities for more freedom and more spontaneity in teaching," which will help us "be more energized and ready to do our work. That, in turn, makes for a better environment for both us and our students" (2). Though we cannot control the wider environment of inadequate classrooms and increasing student numbers, it is encouraging to think that we can create hopefulness in ourselves and our students simply by entering class more mindfully.

2. Sustaining class

A) LAUGHING

When I was new to teaching I would sometimes make jokes about my nervousness because I found it went away when I spoke about it; I would tell my students that I had read that adrenaline keeps you young and that I was actually ninety-five years old. (As this gets closer to the truth, it seems less funny.) My students would also, rather disconcertingly, laugh when I wasn't intending to be funny. I think my British accent and word choice ("I need a rubber!") must have reminded them of TV comedies. Although I have now learned all the Canadian terms, I don't mind that my normal voice is amusing. Humour in class is not necessarily a matter of telling jokes (I always screw up the punchline), but rather is a matter of not taking ourselves too seriously. In moderation, humour can ease tension and improve student learning. There are now numerous articles on the use of humour in the classroom, and recent research in positive psychology helps to explain why it works. Richard Weaver and Howard Cotrell present us with a ten-step program: "A Systematic Sensitization Sequence Designed to Help Instructors Become More Comfortable Using Humor in the Classroom." Their strategies include "1. Smile/Be lighthearted. 2. Be spontaneous/natural. a. Relax control a little/ break the routine occasionally. b. Be willing to laugh at yourself/don't take yourself so seriously. 3. Foster an informal climate/be conversational and loose" (170). I have found a really low-tech method that works well: drawing stick figures on the board not only generates laughter – I am *terrible* at drawing– but also allows me to illustrate a concept more slowly as we unfold the theory. I have proof that students in my class in literary theory remember Louis Althusser's conception of how the subject is interpellated by ideology after seeing my version of a British bobby hailing a poor unsuspecting "subject" with "Hey! You there!" I guess post-Marxism really can create social solidarity.

Positive emotions in an academic context are linked, as we have seen, "to social relationships" (Beard et al. 638). Laughter can promote social harmony, as long as it is not derisive. Jaak Panksepp (who coined the term "affective neuroscience") argues that the adult "taste for humor" originates in childhood: children loved to be chased and tickled because it "arouses the brain" and promotes bonding. Adult laughter "is most certainly infectious and may transmit moods of positive social solidarity, thereby promoting cooperative forms of social engagement" (184).

I recall only one professor in my entire student career who truly enjoyed his classes and made us laugh with him. He brought out the raunchy and colloquial Chaucer, and I still remember being electrified by his evident relish. Another professor – whom we all loved – always read her lectures at top speed, explicitly so that we could get away early. (I was the only student who wanted to go back to the library.)

b) LISTENING

Some years ago a simple question in one of my undergraduate classes generated a strong reaction. The ninety-nine students who were usually talkative were very quiet; I re-posed my question about the poem we were discussing – and still nothing. "What's up?" I asked; I had to repeat the question because there was a stunned silence. We were nearing the end of term. "Do you have many essays to write?" I added. What surprised me most about this class was the reaction. I heard about sick roommates, missing home, the stress of tests, and constant colds. At the end of class I was surrounded by people saying "Thank you for listening," "Thank you for noticing that we are there – or, rather, when we are not." I received more emails later thanking me for caring. It made me quite glum to realize that we often plough on no matter what's going on in the room.

O'Reilley suggests that listening helps us as well as our students: "I do not know why the act of paying acute attention changes the dynamics of a situation, but I can say without reservation that it does" (49). Listening is an important inducement to learning. Carl Rogers's famous student-centred pedagogy has been misappropriated, Blackie et al. argue, in the name of online course delivery. Student-centred learning aims to increase student control over learning. But for Rogers "the essence of the facilitation" is "the personal relationship between student and teacher": "In the absence of the personal relationship, such as in programmatic technology-driven curricula, learning is far less meaningful." The student-centred teacher is actively present. Furthermore, she shows "positive regard" for her students "regardless of whether they are successful at one's subject or not" (Blackie et al. 639). If this smacks of either saintliness or indifference, all we really need to do – as I discovered on that day near the end of term – is listen.

3. Preparing for class

A) PACING

Boice suggests that we "smile, wryly" while preparing classes (*Advice* 41). I was going to end this section here – enough said – but Boice also made me aware that I cannot enter class calmly and enjoy a well-paced, intelligible discussion if I prepare frantically and anxiously: "We wait too long and then binge at the preparation, sometimes in great marathons. This way of working is not only inefficient and unhealthy; it is also self-perpetuating as well as self-defeating" (*Advice* 39). My favourite of Boice's "Eight Rules for Working at Teaching with Moderation" are "1. Wait, patiently and actively 2. Begin early, before feeling ready 3. Prepare and teach in brief, regular bouts 4. Stop, before diminishing returns set in" (*Advice* 18). Boice is so convincing about the beneficial effects of observing these rules that I wonder why we don't all adopt them; he claims it's because they require practice and self-discipline, but I wonder whether it's because we feel guilty when work is enjoyable. If we can actively wait before preparing, we can engage in pre-preparation or the playful sketching out of ideas; if we can begin before feeling fully ready, we don't need to feel certain about what we will do; if we can stop in a timely fashion, we can reflect on how best to present our ideas. Boice claims that "The hard part of active waiting is the patience required, first to wait and reflect and prepare ideas and other material for teaching without insistence that the task be finished in one sitting, second to suspend work on a class preparation to do more with it the next day, while imagining during the interim how it will engage students as active learners" (*Advice* 19). We need to wait "even longer when looking for ideas," says Boice, advocating "patience and tolerance" – with ourselves above all:

> Be playful and optimistic when you can't think of something immediately by giving yourself hints and guessing at the answer in writing. Freewrite or rewrite. Use breaks, reflections, and brief work sessions to keep yourself fresh and on track. Imagine the good, the fun, and the excitement that will come when you present what you are preparing. (*Advice* 41)

B) NARRATING

I have attended workshops over the years on course design, meaningful assessment, and teaching large classes, but somehow I continue to feel overwhelmed when designing a course or planning a new version of one. My autonomic nervous system gears up for teaching all the texts the next day. I continually shuffle things around in an attempt to find a logical progression to the texts, give students enough time to do the readings, avoid new material in a heavier work week, and achieve an appropriate pace.

This year my anxiety was increased by the administration requiring "Learning Outcomes" on syllabi. I felt smug that I came up with some last year, but now – having taught the course – they seem full of irony. Should I promise the student, "You will be a critical reader and thinker who can communicate effectively in oral and written form" (UDLES: University Degree Level Expectations)? Or repeat a version of my course description for Literary Criticism and Theory: "You will: 1) understand – and not be intimidated by – the language of theory; 2) have a knowledge of the main theories which influence how we read literature"; and so on? One of our teaching fellows included the caveat: "On successful completion of this course you will ... " But this caution still does not solve the problem of learning outcomes as quality assurance. As Collini puts it so devastatingly in *What Are Universities For?*, such mechanisms "must translate complex and elusive human achievements into some kind of measurable 'data'":

> Consider, for example, the now familiar phrases about how universities must "assure" the "delivery" of the syllabus, and so on. There is no need to dwell on the more obvious discrepancies between an education and a pizza to recognise here the dangers of encouraging the users of such language to treat a syllabus, and students' engagement with it, as something inert, something that is simply handed over on the doorstep of their minds. (107)

Perhaps we can temper the course as commodity with the course as story. What would it look like and how would it increase our own and our students' enjoyment? Those of us in the humanities are familiar with narratives, but there is increasing recognition in other disciplines of the "way humans construct knowledge ... through story collecting and story telling" (Frisch and Saunders 167). One study of the use of narrative by four different teachers of introductory college-level biology showed not only that students felt "more comfortable around instructors" who used stories, and "more engaged" by the course, but also half of them "reported that stories helped them remember concepts" (168, 167). It was not necessary for students to recall the detail, only that it caused them "to think during lecture." The scenarios that students could recall in detail were either "humorous in tone or surprising," leading the researchers to recognize that "emotions" help students "remember stories and the concepts they teach" (168).

We can tell stories in a course, but we can also tell the course as a story. Since we are all captivated by narratives, Searle-White and Crozier suggest that we conceptualize "the process of teaching as storytelling" (8). It is not difficult, they point out, to discover what is "dramatic" in any subject: "All that you have to do is think of [the lesson] as a story that you will help unfold for the students" (9). A narrative "is simply a description of a situation, a change that happens to that situation, and the result of that change" (8). For me, thinking of and designing my course as a narrative gives it coherence and logic, and enables me to see the overarching theme to which all the parts relate. Teaching dramatizes our subject and our passion for it. Stories are "satisfying," say Crozier and Searle-White, when we "take ideas and unite them with feeling" (8).

Storytelling is not lecturing; it is, rather, "embodied narrative." The storyteller adapts (nuance, pace, detail) as she goes along in response to the students' reactions; in other words, the listeners "need to be able to participate in creating the story" and the instructor needs to be "willing to let the current intellectual, physical and emotional state of the students affect the way she or he teaches" (10). This conception of "embodied narrative" is the difference between "live teaching and learning from a book" (10). I would add that though technology may be able to deliver narrative, it cannot capture the "dynamic give-and-take" (9) of storytelling. This dynamic takes place in a relationship in which the teacher "will be influenced by the energy of the moment and what the needs and interests of the class are," and "students will resonate with what is really happening with the teacher" (11). Frisch and Saunders found that the stories were the part of the biology courses "that students are eager to share with family and friends." As one participant in the case study put it, "stories are what you take with you" (168).

c) INTERCEPTING

Until last year I did not have a "classroom etiquette" on my course schedule, but I found that announcing a policy on the first day of classes has little real effect. When I first started teaching I was offended by students whispering or reading the newspaper, but now it is impossible to distinguish the learning technology from the learning distractions. Last term I became demoralized by one particular student who seemed addicted to texting: she even checked her phone while waiting for her classmates to respond to her seminar presentation. (I called for a break and pointed out that using her phone did not give a good impression.) I talked to her three times about this, and she even said, "I don't live far from campus. I could leave it at home for your class." I now have explicit policies on cell-phone use on my syllabus. Next term I will add a policy on laptop use. Faria Sana et al. conducted compelling experiments that found not only that multitasking on a laptop has detrimental effects on the user's performance but has greater detrimental effects on those around him or her (24–31).

The addicted texter in my class finally did leave her phone at home in a subsequent course and became an enthusiastic participant; she told me that she had only been checking the time. Regina Conti argues that since highly motivated people have "skills and habits" to achieve flow (the state of focused attention discussed in chapter one), "One of these habits is likely to be a tendency to forget about time. Reducing one's attention to time may therefore be an important, yet previously overlooked, means of promoting flow" (21).

4. Marking

Marking assignments is the least enjoyable part of my work; I frequently get stomach ache. O'Reilley's reaction is similar, though less severe: "one of the first things I noticed was how much unacknowledged physical tension I was bringing to the task" (74). Perhaps the way to reduce the stress of marking is to ensure that assignments are not just tools for evaluation but rather are useful and enjoyable for the students themselves. My colleague Sue Fostaty-Young once observed to me that as far as students are concerned the assignments *are* the course; Therese Huston writes that "students learn on the basis of what *they* do in your course, not on the basis of what *you* know" (60).

I have found that allowing students to follow their own interests results in far more interesting and, frequently, fascinating papers, and far fewer instances of plagiarism. Richard Ryan and Edward Deci would say that this strategy fosters students' "intrinsic motivation." The differences between "people whose motivation is authentic (literally, self-authored or endorsed) and those who are merely externally controlled" are quite astonishing: the former have more "interest, excitement and confidence, which in turn is manifest both as enhanced performance, persistence, and creativity ... and as heightened vitality ... self-esteem ... and general well-being" (69).

Conclusion

There are some instructive parallels between Bill Readings's focus on "the scene of teaching" to rescue us from the "University in Ruins," and the Slow Food movement's focus on local artisans to "defend the ... pleasures of food under threat from standardisation ... and fast food" (Andrews 17–18). Geoff Andrews shows how the "fast life" to which we are inured is "rooted in the contemporary world of globalisation and the information society" (30). Tara Brabazon in *The University of Google* argues that our current emphasis on "the rapid transfer of knowledge" has reduced the diversity of higher education: "Affirmations of standards may mask an imperative for homogeneity. Education based in Perth *should* be different from that offered in New York, Brighton or Osaka" (208). She notes the recent emergence of theories of *de*globalization: "There is important theoretical and applicable research to be conducted affiliating critical literacy, localism, and deglobalization, rather than a simplistic affirmation of standards, sameness, and homogeneity" (208). Brabazon cites Wittgenstein's observation that globalization has a "contemptuous attitude toward the particular case." Like Brabazon in the context of higher education and Petrini in the realm of food, my ideal pedagogy strives to defend "the local, specific and particular" against (the flattening effects of) speed (Brabazon 208). My fantasy "Manifesto of Pleasurable Pedagogy" would have the same subtitle as that of the first Slow Food Manifesto of 1986: "International Movement for the Defense of and the Right to Pleasure" (Geoff Andrews 29).

Chapter Three

Research and Understanding

Not everything that counts can be counted.

Collini, *What Are Universities For?* 120

I remember as a child happening upon a promotional puzzle competition in a department store and eagerly signing up. I was one of those kids who did not have a lot, and the prospect of a free prize was tantalizing. I don't remember what the prize was and I certainly didn't win it. What I do remember was the awful feeling of panic as I kept looking at how fast the other children were solving their puzzles. And the more I looked at how far along they were, the more I got behind. When the bell rang, I was ashamed at how little I had progressed. I tied for last place. I am not sharing this anecdote for sympathy (I have moved on, thank you, although I do dislike puzzles) but because I find myself revisiting it when I contemplate the current university climate. I am drafting this chapter in May and even now I hear academics (including myself) voice that they fear that the summer is going too quickly. Recently, I found myself having to ask a student if she had read the novel at the heart of the MA research project she was proposing; she replied, "I've read bits of it." And a colleague who has just published her second book and is about to take on a significant service commitment confessed to me that she is worried about next year's annual report which will have "only" conference papers as evidence of ongoing scholarship. These are all symptoms of what medical doctor Larry Dossey terms "time sickness," the "obsessive belief that 'time is getting away, that there isn't enough of it'" (qtd. in Honoré 3). This condition is pervasive among academics and fostered by the corporate university, as we have argued so far. While this "sickness" takes a toll on us as individuals, it also has detrimental consequences for scholarship.

Rebranding scholars as key players in the knowledge economy, the corporate university emphasizes instrumentalism and marketability. Thomas C. Pocklington and Allan Tupper contend that "Canadian universities now prize research that brings new facts to light ... Frontier research has replaced reflective inquiry, a complex process involving disciplined thought about major issues and the quality of existing knowledge, as the dominant concept of university research" (7). Building on Sheila Slaughter and Larry L. Leslie's examination of "*academic capitalism*" (the application of market models to universities) (8), Daniel Coleman and Smaro Kamboureli describe the current research culture in Canada as "*research capitalism*" (Preface xvi), "the intensification ... of the pressure to attract external research funding from governments and corporations ... but also to produce knowledge that is directly applicable to the needs and priorities of the community at large as identified (chiefly) by the private and government sectors" (Preface xiv). Ginsberg puts it more bitingly: "today's captains of erudition" see "the university as the equivalent of a firm manufacturing goods and providing services whose main products happen to be various forms of knowledge rather than automobiles, computers, or widgets" (168). Even if we adopt the more measured tones of Coleman and Kamboureli, the emphasis on the quantifiable, applied, and profitable "runs the risk of flattening out or restricting the kinds of scholarly activities that universities recognize, promote, and reward" (Preface xvi). Janice Newson's analysis of current funding structures in Canada confirms this. For those of us in the humanities and social sciences, it comes as no surprise that we receive a smaller share of the funding pie. Moreover, since the Canadian Foundation for Innovation and

the Canadian Research Chairs Programme "require universities
to organize their priorities around strategically selected focus
areas as determined by their institutional strategic plan, rather
than around, for example, the intellectual and research priorities of their front line researchers and academic units" (Newson
108), it seems clear that since the existing funding structures
do not serve all research interests equally (even within the same
discipline), they shape the research that is undertaken. The increasingly managerial model of research shifts the focus away
from those doing the scholarship and creates faculty compliance with institutional imperatives. (For a full definition of
managerialism, see Newson 101.) We have all seen "the rise
over the past three decades in offices of research services usually staffed by a team of managers, accountants, and public relations officers" (Coleman and Kamboureli, Preface xiv). It is significant that managerialism is often experienced by academics
as diverting their energy and time; for example, Coleman and
Kamboureli note that "high levels of management ... take time
away from actual research" (Coda 265).

Alongside privileging certain forms of knowledge above others, corporatization has engendered a race against time with important consequences for the quality of our working lives and
the quality of our scholarship. Newson, in summarizing the findings of a survey of academics she conducted with Heather
Menzies in 2007 (see Menzies and Newson "No Time to Think"),
writes that "regardless of discipline, career stage or gender, the
overwhelming majority of respondents indicated that they had
less time than in earlier stages of their career for reflective and
creative thinking and that their reading and knowledge of scholarly literature was narrower and more specialized than it used to
be or than they liked it to be" (Newson 121). The changes to
academic labour have increased the expectations of what it
means to be a productive scholar, while simultaneously increasing class sizes and expanding our job descriptions. Faculty is
caught in a paradox. Newson is "convinced that one of the
most pressing priorities of our time is ... space and time for
reflective, evaluative critical thinking" (122). Similarly, Donna

Palmateer Pennee writes that "time" is "our most pressing infrastructural (and personal and political) need" (73). And Coleman and Kamboureli, in the coda to their collection *Retooling the Humanities*, also point to "*time as an infrastructure need for humanities research*":

> Most humanities scholars depend on time more than any other resource to carry out their research, not to mention that there is a direct correlation between time and the quality or significance of knowledge produced ... Research agencies and universities should expand the meaning of infrastructure so that it refers not only to buildings and technical equipment but also to Research Time Stipends and other support systems that can free time. (266)

While I obviously do not disagree with the need for time, the solution that Coleman and Kamboureli posit is not sustainable. Simply put, it is not possible for all scholars to get research time stipends, and so the proposed structural changes will inevitably exacerbate the "class system" of the research culture that Pennee notes elsewhere in the collection. More to the point, the problem with time cannot be solved solely with more time. Time pressure will not be eased with research leaves. Wishing for more time is a kind of collective fantasy. The way out of time pressure is to challenge the corporate clock by thinking through our perception of time and the expectations of productivity that are driving our sense that we don't have enough time. If we think of time only in terms of things accomplished ("done and done" as the newly popular saying goes), we will never have enough of it.

The title of this chapter draws on Stefan Collini's persuasive caution about the language of research and knowledge production. He argues that "It is vital ... to emphasize that the goal of work in the humanities, in particular, is better described as 'understanding' than as 'knowledge'" (*What Are Universities For?* 77): "Publication ... is ... not always a matter of communicating 'new findings' or proposing a 'new theory'. It is often the expression of the deepened understanding which some individual has acquired, through much reading, discussion, and reflection, on a topic which has been in some sense 'known' for many generations" (*What Are Universities For?* 123). He writes that "'Knowledge' is too easily thought of as accumulated stock" (*English Pasts* 237) and instead proposes the language of "nurturing, animating, revising, and extending our understanding" (*English Pasts* 238), while acknowledging that "Any suggestion of resisting this slide into an inappropriately utilitarian vocabulary is likely to look quixotic, and at times down right suicidal" (*English Pasts* 239). It is vital that we take the risk. For us, the Slow movement opens up one possible alternative vocabulary. And while the premise of this book is that an approach influenced by the Slow movement is beneficial to our individual well-being and all aspects of our professional practice, scholarship is under most scrutiny and, consequently, is the biggest source of anxiety (we ask ourselves "am I publishing enough?" whereas we tend not to ask "am I contributing enough to the Committee on Undergraduate Awards?"). The corporate jargon focuses on research "output" above other parts of our work, such as teaching; Coleman and Kamboureli comment that "Teaching and learning ... are increasingly seen as tangential spinoffs from discovery or applied research" (Preface xvi), and the "neglect of undergraduate education" (6) is one of the central points in T.C. Pocklington and Allan Tupper's *No Place to Learn: Why Universities Aren't Working.* Because the corporate university has aggressively made research (of a certain kind) the top priority, it is in this area of our work that many of us are particularly vulnerable to the ways corporate language can, to borrow Collini's apt phrasing, "colonize our minds" (*What Are Universities For?* 95). Also, it strikes me that because research is what gains most visibility in the current university, it offers a particularly fertile site for resistance. We *can* choose how we talk about our scholarship to each other and more publicly. I remember a few years ago reading an interview in my campus publication with a political theorist about his latest book and feeling tremendous relief when he unapologetically stated it took him more than ten years to write. In the climate of efficiency, such public statements are acts of everyday rebellion.

Collini describes current academic life as "distracted, num-bers-swamped, audit-crazed, grant-chasing ... far removed from classical ideals of the contemplative life" (*What Are Universities For?* 19). The Slow movement can get us back in touch with what it means to carry out scholarly work. Instead of "I am produc-ing ...," we might say to ourselves and others, "I am contemplat-ing ...," or "I am conversing with ..." or even "I am in joyful pursuit of ..." Indeed, Maggie's point about the importance of pleasure in teaching is pertinent in the context of scholarship. Slow opens up ways of thinking about research that challenge the corporate ethos. Using the language of Slow connects us to a larger political and social movement. This is helpful in and of itself. A colleague of mine shared that she was able to make the switch to veganism only when she found a community of like-minded eaters. The same principle applies here. Knowing that there is a global movement for slowing down can fuel us, and this is important because challenging the dominant model of research is quite difficult; going against the grain usually is not easy. Slowing down is about asserting the importance of contem-plation, connectedness, fruition, and complexity. It gives mean-ing to letting research take the time it needs to ripen and makes it easier to resist the pressure to be faster. It gives meaning to thinking about scholarship as a community, not a competition. It gives meaning to periods of rest, an understanding that re-search does not run like a mechanism; there are rhythms, which include pauses and periods that may seem unproductive. It al-lows us to shift from worrying about the annual report to think-ing about what is sustainable over the long haul. And the importance of sustainability extends beyond the individual to the robustness of intellectual work as a whole. The Slow Food movement, as we have explained, is motivated in part by the detrimental effects of agribusiness on the environment. The en-vironmentalist politics of the Slow movement provide a meta-phoric way of thinking about the changes to research culture in the corporate university. We might say that the emphasis on the quantifiable, applied, and profitable compromises intellec-tual community (pitting individuals, departments, faculties, and universities in ever stiffer competition) and intellectual diversity. It homogenizes what scholars do and it threatens to make certain forms of inquiry extinct. Environmentalist David W. Orr, in *The Nature of Design: Ecology, Culture, and Human Intention*, juxtaposes "fast knowledge" with that of "slow knowledge": "Fast knowledge is mostly linear; slow knowledge is complex and ecological" (40), "shaped and calibrated to fit a particular ecological and cultural context" with "the aim of ... resilience, harmony, and the preservation of patterns that connect" (39). Nicola Perullo, building on Orr's distinction, likens "fast knowledge" to a "sort of supermarket of thought ... it can easily be reproduced and applied elsewhere: it is a model of standardization and franchising" (19). This "supermarket" model of research is what the corporate university promulgates and what we need to resist. Corporate time speeds up and instrumentalizes research as well as objectifies those who produce knowledge and the "subject" studied. The culture of speed (and its associated values of efficiency, productivity, applicability, transferability) is at odds with an understanding of the ethical dimension of time because it forecloses potential ways of being and knowing. My focus can be summarized as thinking about time in terms of relationship, to myself and others. I vividly remember a colleague's prolific research record celebrated at a university event: "she's a machine," beamed the speaker. I am not commenting here on my colleague's work; rather, I am expressing scepticism about the terms in which the researcher was praised, which reveal how the fast models of mechanization have taken over how we think about scholarship and ourselves. Slowing down is a matter of ethical import. To drive oneself as if one were a machine should be recognized as a form of self-harm (and in our introduction, we include studies which document the connection between escalating expectations of productivity and stress). Furthermore, being machine-like will hardly generate compassion for others. In the previous chapter, Maggie quoted Mary O'Reilley's comment that overwork makes us "hate students" (50). O'Reilley's point can be taken more generally. And while hate is a strong word, overwork certainly makes us jealous, impatient, and rushed. Slowing down, in contrast, is about allowing room for others and otherness. And in that sense, slowing down is an ethical choice.

Parkins and Craig define the "ethics of time" as taking "time for the self and time for the other" (47). I will discuss each of these in turn. What does "time for the self" mean in the context of scholarship? For me, it means a shift from the dominant view of time as linear and quantifiable to time as a process of becoming. That is, rather than thinking of time as an accumulation of "lines on the CV" (a phrase drilled into many of us in grad school), I am trying to think of time as an unfolding of who I am as a thinking being. Broadly speaking, I am trying to shift the focus from the product (the book, the article, the presentation) to the process of developing my understanding. This is not to say that books and articles and presentations don't get written (although there may be fewer of them), but my experience of writing them changes in the sense that shifting my focus in this way eases some of the time pressure. I can keep at the back of my mind Readings's question, which applies to our students as much as it does to us: "How long does it take to become 'educated'?" (25). We tend to think of time as spent and gone. However, thinking of time as "constitutive, a becoming of what has *not* been before" (Parkins and Craig 40) connects us to the scholarship that we do and goes against the corporate model. In his famous *The Courage to Teach: Exploring the Inner Landscape of a Teacher's Life*, Palmer makes the foundational point that "*good teaching cannot be reduced to technique; good teaching comes from the identity and integrity of the teacher*" (10). For Palmer, pedagogy is about "connectedness" (11), and his principle is also relevant to scholarship. Collini reminds us that scholarship is "a *human* activity, and so is inseparable from the people who do it ... the possibilities of extending our understanding depend not just on what we already understand, but also on what sorts of people we have become" (*English Pasts* 237). Scholarly "findings" depend on who is searching; and the searcher in turn is constituted by what she finds. If I take a solely instrumentalist approach to thinking, I become machine-like. And if I become like a machine, I become the neoliberal subject. As Carlo Petrini puts it in *Slow Food Nation*, "Better ... to 'waste' time – not in the sense of discarding it, like everything that is of no use to the disciples of speed – but by taking the time to think, to 'lose yourself' in thoughts that do not follow utilitarian lines: to cultivate the ecology of the mind, the regeneration of your existence" (180).

"Time for the self" is intimately connected to "time for the other" (Parkins and Craig 47); indeed you cannot fully have one without the other. Parkins and Craig note that the "distractedness of fast life may often preclude" our "acknowledgment of otherness – other people, other places, other times" (4). We all know this on an experiential level; for example, responding to a colleague's draft in detail takes time but does not register in the logic of accounting. Being ethical may actually mean being inefficient at times. It's another risk worth taking. Furthermore, there are deep implications for the nature of scholarship as a whole. For Readings, thinking "belongs rather to an economy of waste than to a restricted economy of calculation" (175); it "does not function as an answer but as a *question*" (160). This conception of "the activity of thinking" (Readings 192) – and surely this should be the top item in our job description – runs counter to the corporate university which exhorts us to arrive at an answer to a research question that can be marketed as efficiently as possible. The open-endedness of thinking is connected to an openness to otherness. Readings writes, "the obligation of community ... [is] one to which we are answerable but to which we cannot supply an answer" (187) as "we do not know in advance the nature of our obligations to others, obligations that have no origin except in the sheer fact of the existence of Otherness – people, animals, things other to ourselves – that comports an incalculable calculation" (188–9). I linger here on Readings's references to the non-human animal to illustrate my point about the ethics of Slow scholarly time. Readings goes on to say, "To believe that we know in advance what it means to be human ... is the first step to terror, since it renders it possible to know what is non-human, to know what it is to which we have no responsibility, what we can freely exploit" (189). To answer the question of what it means to be human sets up the very conditions – "an alibi" (189) – for the exploitation of those who do not qualify for human status, a point which lies at the core of animal studies, critical animal studies, and post-humanist theory. The connection I am drawing out here between the open-endedness of scholarly inquiry and an ethical openness to the otherness of the non-human is vividly brought to life in one of Jane Smiley's novels.

Moo, published in 1995, includes non-human agents in its consideration of contemporary university life. When I first read the novel in the late 1990s, it struck me as a particular comment on the plight of universities in the politically and religiously conservative American Midwest having to demonstrate relevance to attract "enormous corporations, potential investors of great big sums of money" (21). Rereading the novel now, Moo University is no longer at a safe distance; it is all too familiar. While sympathetic to all its characters (a cast of undergraduates, professors of various political and religious stripes, administrators, staff, tycoons, local farmers, horses, and, most memorably, a hog named Earl Butz), the novel is unsympathetic to the system at work: it depicts corporatization's effects, ranging from increasing class sizes to loneliness to cutbacks to market-driven research. The novel saves its most biting satire for the environmental consequences of the corporate university; in fact, Smiley has commented that she didn't conceive of *Moo* as a campus novel but rather as an environmental novel (Nakadate 191, 195). Economist Dr Lionel Gift, the highest-paid faculty member at the university, is implicated in the proposed mining project in Costa Rica; Dr Dean Jellinek is dedicated to his "calf-free lactation project" (154); and the university considers an endowed museum "celebrat[ing] the natural history of the chicken as well as the glory of modern chicken processing technology" (245). The novel offers an ethical counterpoint in the character of Earl Butz, the hog who is isolated and confined as a research project. He is often read as symbolic "of a college which loses sight of its function and grows with no coordinating ideas or restraints" (Schaefer 3). But Earl is more than symbol and more than scientific object: Smiley generates enormous sympathy for his life and death. In chapter thirty-six we read Dr Tim Monahan's instructions to his creative writing class: "rewrite the story you have chosen to revise from the point of view of another character" and cautions that it is "risky to choose ... a pet's point of view"; this "trick .... [has] been tried before and ... invariably, failed" (181). Yet this is exactly what the novel pulls off (chapter thirty-seven is pointedly titled "Earl's Opinion"). Earl is a "brain-owning individual" (269). He is a sentient and emotional being with preferences (he likes his pen tidy, he likes to be scratched, he likes toys, he likes the radio) and with distinct memories of "brown crackling leaves" and "sunlit, moist grass" (270). Smiley's novel can be read as a lyrical protest to the values of efficiency, productivity, and marketability, for it opens up the very relationships that the corporate university threatens to shut down, the relationships, going back to Readings, of "obligation" to "Otherness – people, animals, things other to ourselves" (189).

The ethical engagement with animals as subjects, not objects, is one example of what Slow thinking might look like (and it happens to be an area of research of particular interest to both of us), but the point here is a general one: social critique is at risk in the corporate university. Robert Hassan writes that "instrumentalism takes the world largely as given and attempts to find means of living ever more productively and efficiently in it" (229). The shift is one from thinking about "the why" to "the how of things" (Menzies and Newson, "No Time to Think" 92). This is one of the most significant contentions raised in the literature on higher education.

For example, Nussbaum, in *Not for Profit: Why Democracy Needs the Humanities*, fears that if the corporatization of higher education "continues, nations all over the world will soon be producing generations of useful machines, rather than complete citizens who can think for themselves, criticize tradition, and understand the significance of another person's sufferings and achievements" (2). Giroux has written extensively on the corporate university's assault on democracy and dissent. Similarly, Magda Lewis writes that the "commodity of exchange" and the "much recognized intensification of ... academic labour ...

encourages people to efface the real implication of what we know in return for the more 'sellable' quietude produced by not knowing" (20). Moreover, Magda Lewis and Margaret Thornton are persuasive in their respective arguments that corporatization has specific effects on feminism within the academy:

> Since it is primarily as neoliberal subjects that academics are now generally valued, feminist scholars, like their peers, are expected to serve the new knowledge economy rather than critique it. The homologous relation between feminism and critique means that the contraction of a critical space has necessarily also led to the contraction of feminism within the academy. (Thornton 89)

While, as Thornton argues, "It is assumed that technocratic and applied knowledge, delivered as information, does not need to be interpreted; it speaks for itself" (87), the type of knowledge production fostered in the corporate university is deeply ideological. Corporatization "has facilitated the remasculinization of the academy behind a facade of rationality, neutrality, and technocratic knowledge" (Thornton 77). The "undervaluing" of the humanities and social sciences "has a deleterious *gender* component" (Magda Lewis 17).

The corporate university's language of new findings, technology transfer, knowledge economy, grant generation, frontier research, efficiency, and accountability dominates how academic scholarship is now framed both within the institution and outside it. Collini terms this language "Prodspeak" – a perfect coinage conjuring up the pain we feel! This public-language is one we all have learned to speak. Alongside the consistent pressure to operate within it is the frequently held belief that the language somehow is mere window dressing. We all have heard the latter articulated along lines like this: "We have to respond to the request to fit our departmental research interests into the overall university mission. Don't worry, though, it won't actually change what we do. And the sooner we fill out this report, the sooner we can get back to our real work." But the conditions for academic research are being changed in very real ways, and the consequences, as I have tried to explore above, have far-reaching ethical and political implications. Moreover, as Collini puts it so well, "the more we talk the language of Prodspeak the more we have to live by it" (*English Pasts* 240). I think that we collectively have overestimated our ability to not be changed by the public language, to outsmart it, as it were. Lived experience suggests that we are increasingly internalizing the language of "Prodspeak." In the remaining pages of this chapter I chart my attempt to challenge the internalization of corporate language, to alter my own internal dialogue about research (also known as thinking, reading, and writing). What follows is not in the spirit of prescription (to adapt Palmer, good research cannot be reduced to technique); rather the following affirmations are meant to suggest potential ways of slowing down scholarly time. They may seem obvious; indeed, I can't imagine many or indeed any of my colleagues disagreeing with the idea that good work takes time. Yet on the whole, academics don't live by this idea any longer. Affirmations, in general, are ripe for parody (see the nerdy and loveable self-help aficionado in Al Franken's *Stuart Saves His Family*: "I'm good enough, I'm smart enough, and dog-gone it, people like me"). However, the practice of affirmation is grounded in the understanding that while an individual may rationally accept that quality, not quantity, really matters, for this to sink in, to actually believe it in a culture which bombards us with messages to the contrary and a steady stream of demands, is another matter entirely.

1. *Just wait.* Horace recommended waiting nine years between writing and publishing. We know we don't have that kind of time, but still "thoughts take time" (Jönsson 61). We say something like this to the undergraduate student who wants to "get" a thesis statement right then and there in our office, but we need to tell ourselves and each other. We need to admit that speed can produce less than desirable results. I submitted a book manuscript before it was ready mainly because I was anxious about not producing enough. Of course, it was rejected. I took a break and the time necessary for my project, and then it got its happy

ending. Going back to the example of the graduate student I cited at the beginning of the chapter, this particular student wasn't a "bad" student. Far from it. She was trying to juggle taking courses, doing her TA work, and establishing a research program by meeting deadlines for grant applications. She was taking her cue from the culture around her. Graduate students, faced with a scarcity of funding and job prospects, are particularly vulnerable to the culture of speed, and the expectations they face to professionalize are ever on the rise. Collini comments, "making everyone so jittery that they suffer from *publicatio praecox* will no more improve the quality of our intellectual life than a faster 'rate of production' of ejaculations would necessarily improve our sexual lives. It will, for example, make it more difficult, especially for younger scholars, to think of undertaking a major project which might not yield any entries for the annual return for several years to come, but which might when completed be worth far more than a whole CVful of slight articles and premature 'syntheses'" (*What Are Universities For?* 127).

2. *Hello Shadow!* The path to a published article or book or successful grant application often does not run smooth. As one colleague put it, there is always a "shadow CV" – the list of detours, delays, and abandoned projects which we hide. We all have one and we should be more open about it. And alongside the "shadow CV" we need to remember that writing is often a very difficult thing to do and that there will be days when it does not go well. There will be times when the "inner bully" (Rettig 21) is very loud, pronouncing that our ideas are unoriginal, ill-conceived, and rather obvious; that we are overlooking a major shift in the field of X; and that our writing style is unsophisticated. In short, that we are not good enough. Most of us hide these feelings of shame. If we do let it slip that we are struggling, the responses may not always help. I've had colleagues respond that they are being productive and making progress, while others, in a more generous spirit, say, "we all feel like that on some days," but then quickly change the topic. This denial and embarrassment speak to the climate of collective anxiety about productivity. The culture of excellence makes it difficult to admit to struggle.

3. *More is not necessarily better.* Jane Austen wrote "only" six novels (and none very long by eighteenth-century standards), but they are really good. We need to keep in mind Collini's rebuttal to the accounting culture: "we don't *measure* [scholarship]; we *judge* it. Understanding that distinction, really understanding it, is the first step of wisdom in these matters" (*What Are Universities For?* 122). It is harsh but true when Magda Lewis writes that the current university climate "encourages people to over produce the packaging in order to hide the meagreness of the content" (20). And, as Fanghanel points out, "the traditional ways of evaluating quality in the academy – based on peer review and professional judgement anchored in disciplinary tenets – are challenged by performativity approaches that emphasize genericism, efficiency and transparency" (28).

4. *Sometimes more is better.* The "Three Minute Thesis Competition" (first developed in 2008 at the University of Queensland, Australia) is truly a sign of the times: as the website boasts, "An 80,000 word thesis would take 9 hours to present. Their time limit ... 3 minutes." Being succinct is a good thing, of course; as Jonathan Swift commended his friend Alexander Pope: "he can in one couplet fix / More sense, than I can do in six" (49–50). But Pope's poems aren't known for their shortness (*The Dunciad. In Four Books*, after all, clocks in at more than 800 couplets). The point of concision is not really about keeping it short; it's about clarity of expression. Brevity is not a virtue in and of itself. Living in a culture in which the "notion of frictionless, spontaneous truth now governs the conditions for all modes of intelligibility" (Giroux, *Education and the Crisis of Public Values* 104), we need to remember the values of density, complexity, and ideas which resist fast consumption.

5. *Walk to the library.* As Nicholas Carr demonstrates in *The Shallows*, the digital age, while obviously beneficial in many ways, also has a downside. Studies show that rather than increasing the range of references in scholarly work, digitalization has reduced it. I knew this was true of my undergraduates' essays, which are strikingly uniform in their use of secondary sources

(articles that don't have a "full text link available" on the library database don't make it), but I was surprised to read that this aspect of shallowing is pervasive at all levels. James A. Evans, in "Electronic Publication and the Narrowing of Science and Scholarship," shows that "as journal archives came online, either through commercial vendors or freely, citation patterns shifted. As deeper backfiles became available, more recent articles were referenced; as more articles became available, fewer were cited and citations became more concentrated within fewer articles" (398). He thus cautions, "searching online is more efficient and following hyperlinks quickly puts researchers in touch with prevailing opinion, but this may accelerate consensus and narrow the range of findings and ideas built upon" (395). The point isn't to get in and out of the research process as quickly as possible. We need to wander the shelves to see what we will find, to make time for "finding what you ... can't describe in a key-word search" (Solnit par. 3). We need to make time for what Julio Alves calls "Unintentional Knowledge: what we find when we're not looking," and collectively we need to speak up for the importance of the library.

6. *Just read it.* We need to take the time to read things that we don't "have to" read. Just because reading cannot be easily quantified does not undermine its worth. In response to "what did you work on today?" many of us adopt an apologetic tone when we reply, "just some reading." I'm reminded of the famous passage in Jane Austen's *Northanger Abbey* where the narrator vindicates novel writers and readers, and satirizes prevailing cultural standards: "'And what are you reading, Miss – ?' 'Oh! it is only a novel!' replies the young lady; while she lays down her book with affected indifference, or momentary shame" (31). Many of us feel that reading – unless it is directly connected to producing publication – is not really work because it is pleasurable. (I myself have asked, "does reading count as work?") It is so heartening to read Collini in this context. In preparation for a new administrator's tour of various faculties, Collini was asked to model "research" in his office: "Naturally, I brooded a

good deal over just what sort of *tableau vivant* best represented this activity ... Finally, I realized that if I was supposed to represent 'research in the humanities' it was clear what I ought to be doing: I ought to be sitting alone reading a book" (*What Are Universities For?* 146–7). He fantasizes that one year, his annual report will simply put, "Rereading the Complete Works of Henry James with Special Reference to Getting to the End of *The Golden Bowl* This Time" (*English Pasts* 240).

7. *More Moo, please.* While all of us are very good at analysis in our respective fields, we tend not to direct the same level of critical reading to our profession (pressed for time, it is understandable that we tend to stay within our specific research area). Hall urges us to "examine the textuality of our own profession, its scripts, values, biases, and behavioral norms" (*Academic Self* xiv). I have found reading such meta analyses very helpful in getting me to contextualize my own experience (I am not alone) and to make more conscious choices within the very complex institution.

8. *Follow your heart.* This sounds corny, yes, but our writing is at its best when it is driven by genuine curiosity about a problem even if that is not a "hot" topic at the moment. This is particularly important for graduate students. If you are working on a dissertation on George Eliot, and you strategically search for an American writer for comparison only because transnationalism is "big" right now, this approach may not be the best if love of one's subject matters (and we believe it does) and it may not be strategic in the long run as it is very difficult, if not impossible, to predict how long a topic will be in vogue; academic fashion is quite fickle (and, by the way, there is a Slow Fashion movement now, too). Graduate education these days seems to be overly concerned with getting students, even at the MA level, identifying a "field" in which they will situate themselves rather than encouraging them to frame their work as an engagement with a particular text or texts or question. Graduate students, reacting to the climate the university sets for them, are rushing to professionalize, grasping at the language of specialization and

research findings. More and more we find ourselves saying to students about their research projects, "the framework is very *au courant*. What specific texts will you be working with"? Indeed, it is easy to see the ways in which Slow Food's emphasis on the local lends itself to the emphasis on close textual analysis in the Slow Reading movement. Evans, in his article on the effects of digitalization on scholarship, posits that "modern graduate education parallels this shift in publication – shorter in years, more specialized in scope, culminating less frequently in a true dissertation than an album of articles" (398). While what makes a "true dissertation" is unclear, we have certainly observed the growing efficiency and uniformity of graduate education.

9. *And as many say, keep calm and write on.* For the sake of our happiness and the quality of our scholarship, we need to resist the temptation to measure our "output" against that of others and we need to embrace the variety of scholarly trajectories. We have to think of ways to counter what Pennee describes as the "morale deficit in an already demoralized workplace" (68) created in part by a "Cult of Celebrity," "faculty of an earlier generation who have secured serial research grants or the more recent large research grants, particularly of the kind that show multiple partners, quantifiable results, and immediate media opportunities" and who "work under a halo of entitlement in the administrative firmament of reward" (67). This is not to take away from those who win grants, but only to remind ourselves that we shouldn't reduce the worth of scholarship to grant money. Pennee coins the term "4A Syndrome" (66) for the debilitating effects of SSHRC designating projects as "worthy" of funding but not worthy enough: "How many times do you need to be told that your proposed research is 'good enough but not funded' before you become too demoralized to try again?" (66). And what about those projects that are ranked even below 4A? Are they still worth doing? Clearly the answer to this is yes, or it should be. I know of several influential books which were deemed "not worth funding" but were written anyway. And we need to keep at the top of our minds

"the politics of research funding" (Magda Lewis 19) outlined earlier in this chapter.

"The neoliberal agenda," as argued by Fanghanel among many others, "stands at odds with ideals of discovery, enquiry and intellectual advancement that academics may attach to the research endeavour" (82). Connected to the imposition of neoliberal ideology on research culture is a dramatic decrease in collegial culture, which we explore in the following chapter. Both become mutually supporting. As academics become more isolated from each other, we are also becoming more compliant as resistance to the corporatization of the academy *seems* futile.

Chapter Four

Collegiality and Community

Universities ... should model social excellence as well as personal achievement – teach, by the very way they conduct their own internal business, something about our dependence upon and need for one another, something about how to achieve the feelings of acceptance and encouragement that community life affords, the sense of self-worth and belonging that keeps us all going on the inside.

Tompkins, "The Way We Live Now" 19

In *The Resilient Practitioner*, Thomas Skovholt and Michelle Trotter-Mathison make the case that "psychological wellness" is "an ethical imperative" (166) for those in the helping professions: "Self-care is not an indulgence. It is an essential component of prevention of distress, burnout, and impairment. It should not be considered as something 'extra' or 'nice to do if you have the time' but as an essential part of our professional identities" (Barnett et al. qtd. in Skovholt and Trotter-Mathison 166). Skovholt and Trotter-Mathison include professors among those in the helping professions. Many academics, undoubtedly, will find it jarring to be grouped under this umbrella term (we did, too). Our surprise hardly is surprising given that in academic culture, it's mind over matter; we are expected to "rise above" whatever is ailing us; and rather than help each other, we're taught to compete with each other. And we are passing this on to the next generation of academics. Many graduate programs have a touch of boot camp; the survivors regale the recruits with war stories. Skovholt and Trotter-Mathison's position that self-care is important not only to personal well-being but also to professional practice is worthy of our attention. Part of the self-care that they advocate is "social support" (182): it is important "to pump positive emotions into" the workplace (183) and to "talk with our colleagues openly and honestly about our work" (182). Yet finding this kind of social support in the academy is becoming more and more difficult. As one colleague relayed to us in a workshop, "the hallways in my department are empty. They weren't when I started. The daily interaction among colleagues is disappearing. Everyone is too busy." Another commented, "no one is in the office. There is no one to turn to for some quick advice about the wording of a sensitive memo, or the selection of a course text." Why are we talking to each other less? Why are so many of us feeling isolated at work? These are important questions. Studies show that loneliness at work "increases attention to negative social stimuli," making people "form more negative social impressions of others" (Cacioppo and Hawkley 450, 452); on the other hand, a sense of community helps members of a unit cope with stress: "people are less likely to appraise potentially stressful events as threatening if they are in a supportive environment" (Shelley E. Taylor 269).

As we have said repeatedly, corporatization has imposed an instrumental view of not only time but also each other. We are enjoined to spend our time in ways that can be measured and registered in accounting systems. Deans' reports tend not to have sections with headings such as "helping a colleague figure out why a lecture didn't go well" or "offering support to an overwhelmed junior colleague" or "expressing enthusiasm for a colleague's new research project." In a climate of accounting, such activities belong to "an economy of waste" (Readings 175) and, given the increasing faculty workload, it is not surprising that they fall by the wayside. Something has to give. As Jane Tompkins notes, "Nobody has time ... You can't put a good conversation on your vita" and as a result, "there's no intellectual life left in universities, or precious little, because people are too busy getting ahead professionally ... to stop and talk to each other" ("Can We Talk?" 21). Many of the texts on time management we surveyed in chapter two actually advise against spending time "just" talking with colleagues. Yet talking to each other is essential. Skovholt and Trotter-Mathison insist that venting is not whining:

> Professional venting ... can be especially important for practitioners who attempt to help people in the human services, education, or health care. Practitioners hear stories of distress. They
> · need to motivate individuals for change when internal motivation is limited, and they often work in an environment of loss, anxiety, and pain. At work, counsellors, therapists, teachers, and health professionals live in an ocean of distress emotions. Their willingness to work in this ocean is a big part of why they get paid. (184–5)

While certainly not every classroom is an "ocean of distress emotions," many are most definitely full of mixed emotions: joy, excitement, fear, boredom, anger, anxiety. And sometimes we do encounter distress in our offices: the student who is going through a break-up; the student whose mother is dying; the student who is furious with her "B," which will keep her from getting into medical school. And then there is our disappointment when we open the email that rejects the manuscript we have been working on for years. But who do we turn to at those crucial times?

Alongside altering our sense of academic time, corporatization has brought increasing workloads and changed the structure of academic appointments. Contingent labour is ever on the rise, and, conversely, so is the star system of research funding. Academics are encouraged to take an entrepreneurial approach to their work, to be ready to leverage their assets, and to be as upwardly mobile as possible rather than "tied" to a specific campus. Those of us in contractual positions are particularly vulnerable to isolation. A few years ago on a hiring committee, one of us reviewed a letter of application from someone who was already teaching as a sessional in her department – and she had never heard of him!

In *Fast Food Nation*, Eric Schlosser writes, "the fast food industry has helped to transform not only the American diet, but also our landscape, economy, workforce, and popular culture. Fast food and its consequences have become inescapable, regardless of whether you eat it twice a day, try to avoid it, or have never taken a single bite" (3–4). This transformation is certainly visible in our universities and colleges. Giroux remarks that "as higher education is corporatized ... campuses ... look more like malls" ("Attack" 16). They also feel like malls. Many, if not most, of us now just run into our departments to grab our mail or attend a meeting and then leave as quickly as we can. Increased use of technology makes it possible for us to do so. Academic rituals that were conceived of as community building are on the decline. Doctoral dissertations are examined via teleconference, and this method is welcomed as cost-effective and efficient. And even the academic conference is threatening to become a long-distance relationship. At a recent conference we both attended, one of the plenary speakers delivered his address via Skype because, as he readily admitted, he had mixed up his dates. There were the predictable technical difficulties making it very difficult to hear the paper, and there was no opportunity to talk with him. The fact that the lecture wasn't just cancelled (the schedule already was packed) seems to suggest that in this age of connectivity, actual connection is optional. Sherry Turkle's book *Alone Together* sums up this idea: "Networked, we are together, but so lessened are our expectations of each other that we feel utterly alone. And there is the risk that we come to see others as objects to be accessed – and only for the parts we find useful, comforting, or amusing" (154).

It has been argued that the decline of the university club is symptomatic of the corporatization of higher education. In the current climate of economic austerity, it is unlikely that resources will be allocated to bring back the university club. Moreover, it is doubtful that the existence of this building would solve the problem we are identifying. In the "new regime" of connectivity,

we are losing our place; the campus is now a "place of social collection" (Turkle 155): "a 'place' used to comprise a physical
space and the people within it. What is a place if those who are
physically present have their attention on the absent?" (Turkle
155–6). The Slow movement urges us to immerse ourselves in
local cultures, but our home departments are on the verge of
becoming ghost places. The hallways are empty because we work
elsewhere, and we work elsewhere because the hallways are empty. Even departmental "business" no longer brings us together.
Much of discussion has shifted to email or web forums, and when
a meeting is called, people are "there but not there" (Turkle 14).
As Turkle puts it, "in the world of paper mail, it was unacceptable
for a colleague to read his or her correspondence during a meeting. In the new etiquette, turning away from those in front of you
to answer a mobile phone or respond to a text has become close
to the norm" (161). Indeed, we have observed texting at department meetings, retirement events, and graduation ceremonies.
What is this about? Zygmunt Bauman suggests,

> The latent function that mobile phones have and email sorely
> misses is that they enable the talkers to opt *out* of the place in
> which they are bodily immersed at the moment .... In addition,
> however, they offer the talkers the facility to make their unattach-
> ment manifest and publicly known where and when it truly counts
> .... it makes it obvious that face-to-face contacts bear a secondary
> importance. (qtd. in Franklin 347)

Indeed, when a colleague turns to answer a text when talking to
us, it is difficult to feel that we matter. Shelley E. Taylor points
out that "social support is the perception or experience that one
is cared about by others, esteemed and valued, and is part of
a social network of mutual assistance and obligations" (265).
Turkle suggests that the turn to electronic communication has
to do with fear – it is more difficult to control in-person communication. Even a telephone call is more risky because less contained than text or email (Turkle 187–9, 206). "We'd rather text
than talk" (Turkle 1) – even, or should it be especially, if the

person is down the hall. Turkle's analysis rings true particularly at this time when the atmosphere in the academic workplace is one of demoralization, overwork, and competition. The display of detachment, the opting out, which the mobile phone facilitates, as explained by Bauman, is both symptomatic of the culture of busyness and a defensive response to it.

Turkle, near the end of her book, shares her dismay at seeing someone text at a funeral. When she raised it with friends, "several shrugged. One said, 'What are you going to do?'" She goes on to say, "A shrug is appropriate for a stalemate. That's not where we are. It is too early to have reached such an impasse" (296). One of us received the same response when raising the issue of texting at department meetings; a sympathetic colleague said, "it's annoying, I agree, but what are you going to do?" What we need to do is talk about it. We need to attend to how we feel when someone does take the time to be fully present. Those instances of generosity and true connection can guide us to thinking critically about the current university climate's toll on human relationships. As Turkle writes in her cautionary tale about the limitless and exciting potential of technology, "when we ask what we 'miss,' we may discover what we care about, what we believe to be worth protecting" (19).

There is a growing recognition that we are losing a sense of collegiality but an uncertainty about how to bring it back. Part of what makes talking about collegiality difficult is the way the concept can be deployed punitively. Collegiality has been used as a smokescreen for discrimination in tenure and promotion decisions. Certainly Boice's recommendation to new faculty epitomizes the chilling effect: "you need only the appearance of aloofness and uncooperativeness" to "fail because of social problems" (*Advice* 203). Collegiality can compromise academic freedom and turn into homogeneity: some advice books even go so far as to recommend that you dress like your colleagues. This chapter is not about adding collegiality (or dress code) as a criterion to teaching, research, and service in assessments of an individual's work; nor is it about coming up with a rubric such as the Collegiality Assessment Matrix of "*observable behaviours*"

(Cipriano and Buller 46), which include "stepping up when needed" and "meeting deadlines" (Cipriano and Buller 47). But we do agree with Linda Hutcheon that in spite of "the problems of using collegiality as a subjective criterion in the professional evaluation of individuals," we should "not abandon the very real positive advantages – in intellectual as well as human terms – of collegiality as a collective ideal and reality" (63). In *Junior Faculty Development: A Handbook* published by the Modern Language Association in 1991, Donald Jarvis reports the following findings from his survey of over one hundred faculty members at eight universities and colleges in the U.S. In response to the question "What do you believe should be done to best develop young faculty members?" 89% identified collegiality, outranking all other considerations such as resources and training (Jarvis 110). Sixty-three percent of respondents regarded collegiality as the most important factor in their professional development (Jarvis 112), while for "generat[ing] ideas," 44% of respondents cited collegial exchange, which was surpassed only by reading (51%) (Jarvis 116). Lack of collegiality was regarded by 50% as detrimental to professional development (Jarvis 114). These percentages show how much collegiality matters.

Hall's *The Academic Self* and *The Academic Community* both tackle the issue of collegiality and recommend the setting up of works-in-progress series, speaker events, retreats, and reading groups. These solutions, which are representative of advice on the topic, "cost nothing except for time and commitment ... Even on the cheap it is still possible to offer colleagues many opportunities to invest themselves in their community" (*Community* 96). These words are meant to be encouraging but they have the opposite effect and highlight the problem inherent in the literature on collegiality. How can it take "only" time and energy, when those are precisely what we are running low on? Hall is confident that if we schedule service and community building into our weeks, alongside our teaching and writing (*Self* 82), community will emerge. But as we explored in chapter one, daytimers are not the answer. In keeping with self-help discourse, Hall emphasizes personal responsibility, but personal responsibility can also slide into blame: he writes, for example, "just because someone else is reneging on his or her responsibility does not let you off the hook" (*Self* 69) and "if we are unhappy with the atmosphere in our departments, if we find that our communities suffer from intellectual or pedagogical inertia and other dysfunctions, then, as members of that community, we are partially responsible for that atmosphere" (*Community* 86).

It is clear by now that we believe in individual agency, but we are wary of neglecting to take into account the institutional and political factors which set the conditions for our work; the campus is not a level playing field where one dean's "reneging" can be made up for by a junior faculty member's "stepping up." Moreover, even if (and it's a big if these days) we find the time and energy for works-in-progress, speakers, retreats, and reading groups, these strategies do not come with guarantees. They will succeed only if generated from positive emotions; otherwise they become further occasions for the negative emotions attending competitiveness and even fear.

When a colleague suggested to one of us a course in which the same text is taught by a group of instructors sitting in on each other's lectures, for the pedagogical purpose of allowing students to see the range of critical perspective and the collegial purpose of allowing faculty to see what each other does, her immediate response was one of horror – not that she expressed that of course. She mumbled something about it being an interesting idea but institutional constraints might make implementation difficult. Similarly, faculty members have confessed to us that they are more nervous about presenting at a works-in-progress than at the MLA. That we fear speaking to our colleagues deserves our attention. Before we can put into practice a regime of speaker events, we need to address the climate of isolation which pervades current academic life. As Tompkins writes, structural changes will not "automatic[ally]" produce collegiality "without some prior attention to the social and emotional dimensions of talk" ("Can We Talk?" 29).

We are claiming that a university club can be empty, a works-in-progress series can confirm divisions in a fractured department, and social gatherings can be reduced to opportunities for self-promotion. Even well-meaning advice in the current climate is in danger of turning collegiality into the exchange of marketable skills. Seeing colleagues as resources precludes the affective dimensions of talk, turning others into sound bites. Susan Robinson in *The Peak Performing Professor* offers a chapter on how to "Engage Others" and then on how to "Collaborate for Mutual Benefit." She advises those of us who are shy to attend social functions with a clear idea of "what outcomes ... you want" from the event (142); keeping our eye on the goal will motivate us to greet people, remember names, begin conversations, and ask questions. Robinson suggests that we counterbalance a colleague's reserve by asking questions, and after listening to "a few sentences, summarize what the person has said so far using active listening" (156). We cannot imagine a more irritating interlocutor, but Robinson assures us that practice will enable us to offer more creative synopses; only years of experience could come up with a line like this: "So you really like what you have been working on this year but you want to produce more publications in the next two years" (156). We could save ourselves the trouble of listening by memorizing this one-size-fits-all response for the next faculty function. To expand our network of colleagues, Robinson suggests keeping a database with "a subfile of people who can help" with a project. We will need to "clean" up this file "from time to time eliminating contacts who are not relevant to the goal of mutual support" (154). We should not be lulled by the metaphor of "villages" for groups of colleagues: we are advised to "mine the gold of your own village" while also "occasionally targeting" other "villages" (155). This military-industrial language illustrates the fact that viewing collegiality as a live version of virtual networking burdens it with the latter's alienation and objectification. Apart from the chill that we may be on someone's subfile (or worse, eliminated for being unhelpful and irrelevant), this confirms Adrian Franklin's insights on the connections between social loneliness and the use of social media.

Franklin, quoting Bauman, argues that virtual networking has infected social life: "'network' stands for a matrix for simultaneously connecting and disconnecting; networks are unimaginable without both activities being simultaneously enabled" (346). In networking, "connecting" always already implies "disconnecting," so that in place of relationships we have affiliations which can be "entered into on demand and can be broken at will" (346). Franklin points out – through Bauman – that current levels of social loneliness are charged by "fear of immanent disposal." Consumerist society "has changed the way we organize our individualism"(345): "everything, including relationships, is aestheticized and evaluated in terms of its capability to offer beauty, desire and pleasureability" (354); relationships are understood to be "until further notice" (344). Franklin is less "surprised" than Coget et. al. by their finding of "a positive, significant correlation between online socializing and loneliness" (Franklin 350). It seems clear to us that attempting to achieve collegiality by transferring the model of virtual networking to face-to-face encounters only alienates us even further. Conversation is instrumentalized, and colleagues are turned into "either resources or hindrances" (Martela 80).

Proposed solutions to workplace isolation that focus on the individual are doomed to fail because it is fundamentally a social phenomenon. Both loneliness and belonging are contagious. VanderWeele, Hawkley, and Cacioppo discovered that "the number of days an individual was lonely each week was found to influence the levels of loneliness of friends, neighbours, and spouses" (781). Like the upward spirals of emotional contagion discussed in chapter two, workplace loneliness forms part of a downward spiral: "Loneliness not only spreads from person to person within a social network, but it also reduces the ties of these individuals to others within the network" (Cacioppo and Hawkley 452).

A project focused on teacher burnout concluded that "negative emotions appear to be more contagious than are positive emotions" (Bakker and Schaufeli 2291). A research study at the University of Toronto found that this automatic emotional conductivity manifests as actual coldness. Estimates of room temperature and increased need for warm drinks were directly tied to the experience of social exclusion: "the experience of loneliness is often accompanied by the perception of reduced ambient temperature" (Zhong and Leonardelli 839), leading the researchers to claim that metaphors of psychological coldness (the "icy stare") originate in visceral experience. They conclude that "controlling ambient temperature may ... be a relatively inexpensive and nonintrusive way to restore group cohesiveness and prevent damage due to interpersonal friction" (841). But since warm hallways are still empty hallways, we would prefer to think that we could lower the heating costs of the university and reduce our carbon footprint by being warm to each other.

While we believe that strong social support is vital to the successful running of the university and our educational mission within it, we would like to suggest a shift in how we conceive of collegiality. Emphasizing the affective aspects of collegiality may intervene more successfully in our current feelings of isolation. Frank Martela offers a new and, we believe, more constructive way to think about collegiality. He points out that existing research on well-being at work focuses on employees' cognitive assessment of the characteristics of their jobs or on how they manage their own well-being. The problem is that this "individualistic and rationalistic paradigm ... downplays and marginalizes the role of feelings and emotions as well as human relationality" (82). In this model, emotions are the "enemies of reason," a threat to organizational life. Yet when people are asked about their jobs, they do not generally talk about what they actually do "but rather about ... the feelings they experience in their encounters" with others (Sandelands and Boudens, qtd. in Martela 84). Job satisfaction, in other words, is experienced and "construed in affective terms" (Martela 85).

We need to recognize, then, that well-being "takes place intersubjectively, between people, rather than being an individual achievement" (Martela 82). How would this alter our approach to the issue of collegiality in the present-day university? First, we should not assume that the empty hallways mean that it's all over. Collegiality needs to be seen as "an ongoing social accomplishment ... rather than something fixed and final" (Martela 85). It is, as Martela points out, oriented towards the future, "emergent and co-constructed" (86), a matter not of "well-being" but of "well-be(com)ing" (85). Rather than addressing individual members' lack of social skills, we need to see the workplace as "a kind of holding environment" or "supporting net" (85, 97). Martela's research on caregivers in a large public nursing home revealed "a network of interpersonal relationships that together give rise to group-level, systemic processes that are not reducible to individual members" (86). Clearly, this is a very different use of the term network: a good "holding environment" is able to contain fluctuations in its members' emotions, allowing for the expression of negative as well as positive feelings. This reminds us of Skovholt and Trotter-Mathison's insistence that venting is not whining. The practical characteristics of a "well-functioning team" are "asking and giving advice, helping each other out, sharing the workload fairly, knowing each other's strengths and weaknesses, and trusting each other" (Martela 97). These activities of mutual support depend upon, indeed cannot be separated from, the "emotional dimension" Martela identifies: "respecting each other, sharing emotional burdens, encouraging each other, knowing each other as a person, and solving emotional problems together" (97). This is a far cry from reading groups and works in progress. It may well be that an effective (and affective) "holding environment" requires as much work as team teaching, but it is a different kind of work.

The first step to creating a "holding environment" is to acknowledge that workplace loneliness is real. This in itself is an act of courage because, as Franklin puts it, loneliness "would 'rather not' speak its name" (343). Moreover, a person's loneliness is not the result of his/her deficiency in social intelligence; studies which offer to fix the individual's social skills are misplaced. Nor is a fractured climate the result of individuals failing their responsibilities. Second, we have to acknowledge "that the workplace is populated by people who have social and emotional needs both outside of work *and* during work hours" (Wright 140). We can't fix workplace loneliness by telling ourselves to find more rewarding activities outside of work in hopes of diminishing its role in our lives; sidestepping the issue isn't the answer. With the rise of work hours coupled with the decline of traditional communities, "the role of the work community as a fulfiller of this basic human need [of interpersonal attachment] has increased":

> We ... need work communities that are communities in the true meaning of the word – recognizing us also on the affective and relational levels. Yet the rationalistic-bureaucratic understanding of working life that ignores and even consciously downplays this dimension still dominates much of our thinking about organizational life. (Martela 106)

The corporate and remasculinized university dismisses turning inwards and disavows emotion in pursuit of hyper-rational and economic goals.

This is why practical suggestions such as Hall's that we add community building to our agendas, or Robinson's that we maintain a database of useful contacts, only make the hallways more chilly. Conceived as active networking, collegiality is in danger of being distinctly uncongenial. Yet it is vitally important that we recognize that workplace loneliness affects our well-being, interferes with professional development, and makes us more vulnerable to burnout. A supportive environment, on the other hand, can actually reduce our perceptions of the stresses caused by even the most recalcitrant corporate context: "Social support may be particularly beneficial for helping people to manage job demands that are not easily modified through organizational structures or change" (Shelley E. Taylor 270). Yet collegiality should not be onerous. Creating a "holding environment" requires the simple acknowledgment that our work has a significant emotional dimension, whether it be disagreeing with a colleague in a meeting, or finding a student guilty of a departure from academic integrity. Admitting to the affective impact of our responsibilities constitutes what Skovholt and Trotter-Mathison call venting as opposed to whining: the former engenders mutual support, the latter increases feelings of helplessness. In the corporate climate collegiality is worth nurturing; as Shelley E. Taylor documents, it may actually save our lives: "The effect of social support on health is as powerful or more powerful than well-established medical predictors of chronic disease and death. For example, social support is more important than blood pressure, lipids, obesity, and physical activity in predicting cardiovascular-related health outcomes, and it is on a par in magnitude with smoking" (267).

The original version of this chapter did not include practical advice. Whereas an individual can shape her own teaching and research, community obviously cannot be created alone. There is a degree of autonomy in teaching and research, but none in collegiality. Second, community is intangible and fluid, making it much more difficult to offer practical solutions. However, since one of our anonymous readers expressed disappointment at their absence, we endeavour here to offer some themes for reflection.

If you want an event to be joyless, make it mandatory. Collegiality cannot be legislated. Speaker events can often feel like yet another thing to do.

If we don't vent, we will begin to whine. The experience of stress lessens when we feel supported. We have found that talking to each other helps us avert the downward spiral into loneliness, suspicion, and burnout.

Risk candour. A "holding environment" is one of mutual trust: we need to take the risks required for intimacy, risk being less than perfect and not always on top of things, and risk caring about each other's well-being and health. It may not always go well; your candour will not be reciprocated every time, but when it is, the rewards are immense.

"Ask what we miss." As Turkle says, "when we ask what we 'miss,' we may discover what we care about" (19). This will be different for each of us. For one of us, it is spontaneously heading to the campus cafeteria with a colleague. For the other, it used to be going into the department knowing that there would be someone to chat with (and now there is).

Don't give up hope. Departmental cultures can change. And there can be subcultures of support within departments creating pockets of resistance to the effects of the corporate university.

Collaboration and Thinking Together

Often, challenges that seem insurmountable when you're trying to accomplish them alone can seem much easier to manage following a word of encouragement and advice.

Shelley E. Taylor 269

Concentrated, inspired conversation is a widely undervalued source of new knowledge, new feelings, new impulses.

Jönsson 52

Exploring the deleterious effect of the changing university climate on collegiality, Jane Tompkins notes that "you can't put a good conversation on your vitae" ("Can We Talk?" 21). While this truth is evident in the empty hallways we explored in the previous chapter, this book (which most definitely is on our vitae) is the result of good conversation. The project began with us talking to each other – a lot – about our experiences as academics. And it's only because of continued conversations with each other and with other colleagues that the book was completed. Talking with others made clear to us that many of us are searching for meaningful exchange about what it feels like to be an academic in the corporate university, and it drove home the fact that the corporate university actively militates against us having these exchanges. Collini, speaking of his essays on the "misconceiving ... of scholarly research" (reprinted in *What Are*

Universities For?), shares that "a larger number of people seem to have been stirred to write to me by reading these ... articles ... than by reading anything else I have ever written, and ... their letters expressed not only support but what I can only call delight – delight that someone had expressed publicly convictions which they deeply shared but which seemed to be having a hard time of it in their own academic institutions" (*English Pasts* 233). Our experience has been similar, and it motivated us to write this book in spite of the inevitable discomfort of going against the grain of institutional cultures.

At the time we were writing, we were also engaged in solitary book projects in our respective fields and the experience was very different. We often remarked to each other that working together has been more pleasurable, more convivial (to use the Slow Food term), than any other project we have ever undertaken. And, even beyond that, both of us feel that we simply wouldn't have been able to do it on our own. As we reflected on the differences between working on this and on individual monographs, some key points emerged. All of them seem to be characteristic of the "holding environment" (Martela 85) discussed in the previous chapter. To liken collaboration to a holding environment resonates with gestures of care and protection. It suggests that the inevitable difficulties that arise will be withstood and that faith will be kept. It offers the promise that ideas will be preserved and nurtured rather than dismissed; academic training makes us good at the latter, but the conventional ideas of "rigour" deserve some scrutiny.

Writing, we all know, can be hard. There are the inevitable and universal challenges which beset everyone: writer's block, procrastination, doubt, fatigue, and guilt. The changes in the university climate have increased the expectations of research "output" while at the same time increasing overall workloads, making it more difficult than ever to set aside time in the face of the more immediate and tangible teaching and administrative demands. We obviously were not immune to these pressures (and our editor can confirm that this book took us longer than planned), but our experience of these pressures was strikingly different from other writing projects due to one simple fact: we were able to talk to each other about them. Doing so meant that we didn't internalize the feelings, or, if we did, not for very long. Working together took away the power of shame. In the New York Times Best Seller *The Gifts of Imperfection*, Brené Brown, a leading researcher on the emotion of shame, defines it as "*the intensely painful feeling or experience of believing that we are flawed and therefore unworthy of love and belonging*" (39). According to Brown, no one escapes this feeling: "we all have it ... The only people who don't experience shame lack the capacity for empathy and human connection." And even though we all feel it, "we're all afraid to talk about shame" and "the less we talk about shame, the more control it has over our lives" (38). To develop "shame resilience" (for there is no cure) requires that we "recognize what messages and expectations trigger shame," "practice critical awareness by reality-checking the messages and expectations," "reach out and share [our] stories with people [we] trust," and "speak ... [and] use the word *shame*" (40). While Brown's book doesn't address academia (although her subsequent *Daring Greatly* mentions university culture as shaming), it is not difficult to translate her definition into a specifically academic context. It might read something like this: "Academic shame is the intensely painful feeling or experience of believing that we aren't as smart or capable as our colleagues, that our scholarship and teaching isn't as good as that of our colleagues, that our comments in a meeting or at a speaker event aren't as rigorous as that of our colleagues, and therefore we are unworthy of belonging to the community of great minds." And shame, as Rettig reminds us, is not good for writing; it actually keeps us from doing it (5–6).

The foundation for the holding environment we were fortunate to experience is trust. We both were warned about collaboration, and we certainly heard many horror stories ranging from frustration about different working styles to perceived exploitation. In fact, we were even warned not to collaborate because we were such good friends. Our experience has proven otherwise. We believe this to be the case because of the trust and

knowledge of each other we had built up over time. We see the
other as the whole person, not as a "position" on an academic
question or as an instrumentalized networking "contact." This
meant that we were more patient with each other and more
compassionate when life events or work pressure intervened in
a deadline. Recognizing that the understanding and care that
we extended to each other brought out the best in us has made
us more compassionate towards our students. We not only motivated each other to keep going but also gave each other permission to see work-life balance as a legitimate goal, a balance
particularly tenuous for academics whose commitment and love
for their subject matter can make drawing the line between work
and life more difficult. And it meant that we genuinely listened
to each other. In *Thinking, Fast and Slow*, Daniel Kahneman comments on his collaboration with Amos Tversky: "one of the great
joys ... was that Amos frequently saw the point of my vague ideas
much more clearly than I did" (6). Working with someone who
will hold on to an idea's potential when fear and anxiety are
threatening to erase it is a tremendous gift, and we each took
turns doing that for the other. And when one of us considered
an idea or sentence as not working, she was able to say so without crushing the other in the way that peer review often does.
The underlying trust and respect made it possible to have an
open exchange of ideas: we listened to each other in an attempt
to understand rather than to find the weaknesses as we had been
trained to do. The result was the same.

Even though our joint writing sessions were interspersed with
individual and solitary work, the presentations we have given
and the book are very much *ours*. There are many parts of the
project (such as the introduction) where we simply cannot recall who said what; we sat together and completed each other's
sentences. Then there are parts of the project (the chapter on
time management) where the initial writing was divided between
us, and then revised together. The chapters on teaching and on
research were largely composed independently. And while we
were delighted by how well they connected to each other, we

found them the most difficult to write. We even recognized that when working independently on those chapters, we turned each other into the "inner bully" (Rettig 21) or imagined reviewers singling out the chapter we were writing on our own as the weakest link. And when one confessed that that's what she was feeling, the other, with relief, burst out, "that's how I feel!"

Given our experience on this project, we would like to suggest that in order for collaboration to work well, it emerges locally in conversations between people, rather than being imposed top-down by funding models. The corporate university puts a high value on research clusters and collaboration, emulating, as Fanghanel puts it, "the Silicon Valley model" (88) of pooling expertise to increase competitiveness on a global scale. If collaboration is turned to in the hope of boosting productivity and streamlining research, it can easily produce resentment between colleagues: one member, justifiably or not, feeling like they're doing "more" than the other(s). Collaboration, it strikes us, is not about "reducing" the work by dividing the tasks. Although this can happen, it's not a motivation that will sustain a project over the long haul. Collaboration is about thinking together. And undertaken in that spirit, collaboration can allow us to challenge neoliberal models of higher education and the remasculinization of the academy. As Kahneman, again speaking of his collaboration with his friend and colleague, puts it so beautifully, "Amos and I enjoyed the extraordinary good fortune of a shared mind that was superior to our individual minds and of a relationship that made our work fun as well as productive" (10). This is thinking together in its best sense.

The conviviality of thinking together protected us from "the damage caused by the fast life" (Petrini, *Slow Food Nation* 182). In retrospect, we realized that writing this book put Slow principles into practice, and we learned that the process was inextricable from the product. Slow philosophy overall should not be interpreted, Petrini reminds us, as "the contrast ... between slowness and speed – slow versus fast – but rather between attention and distraction; slowness, in fact, is not so much a question of duration as of an ability to distinguish and evaluate, with the propensity to cultivate pleasure, knowledge, and quality" (*Slow Food Nation* 183). Distractedness and fragmentation characterize contemporary academic life; we believe that Slow ideals restore a sense of community and conviviality – "friendship and the joining of forces" (*Slow Food Nation* 183) – which sustain political resistance. As envisioned in our manifesto, Slow professors act with purpose, cultivating emotional and intellectual resilience to the effects of the corporatization of higher education.

Acknowledgments

Maggie Berg and Barbara K. Seeber would like to thank the following people:

Brittany Lavery, formerly associate acquisitions editor at University of Toronto Press, for her enthusiasm about this project in its very early days.

Douglas Hildebrand, our current editor, for his patience and for chaperoning us through the complexities of the publication process. Lisa Jemison, managing editor, and Catherine Plear, copy editor, for getting us through the final stages.

The anonymous reviewers for their wonderful comments.

Participants at workshops we have given at Brock, Queen's, St. Mary's, Mount Allison, and the conferences of the Society for Teaching and Learning in Higher Education (STLHE) and the International Society for the Scholarship of Teaching and Learning (ISSOTL). Their responses and encouragement motivated us to keep going.

An earlier version of the book's introduction was published as "The Slow Professor: Challenging the Culture of Speed in the Academy" in *Transformative Dialogues: Teaching and Learning Journal* (6.3 [2013]). We are grateful to the editors for granting us permission to reprint.

Maggie Berg's acknowledgments:

Above all, I want to thank Barbara for her wisdom, humour, honesty, patience, and extraordinary friendship; I would not and could not have written this book without her.

92 Acknowledgments

I would like to thank Queen's University Chairs in Teaching and Learning for its generous support of the project over three years, and Queen's Office of the Vice-Principal (Research) for its contribution to the publication.

Thank you to everyone at Queen's Centre for Teaching and Learning for their support: Sue Fostaty-Young, Andy Leger, Joy Mighty (former director), Denise Stockley, and Susan Wilcox; a special thanks to Sandra Murray.

Thanks also to Karen Donnelly; Ellen Hawman; Brenda Reed; Lally Grauer (I want to get it right this time); Cathy Harland for her lasting friendship and wonderful conversations; Shelley King for her tireless support and exemplary collegiality; Chuck Molson for the great runs; Christine Overall for her invaluable advice; Marta Straznicky for her encouragement; my colleagues for reviving my sense of collegiality; particular thanks to Brooke Cameron, Gwynn Dujardin, Petra Fachinger, Fred Lock, Heather Macfarlane, John Pierce.

Thanks to my students for reminding me why this all matters.

Thanks to: my family in England for the wonderful dinners, the laughter, and the beach huts (and because they will appreciate Mater/Gran's advice); Scott Wallis for always listening, always knowing the right thing to say, and always doing the dishes; Rebecca Barrett-Wallis for being the most lovely person I could ever have imagined.

Barbara K. Seeber's acknowledgments:

First of all, I am so grateful to my friend Maggie for her honesty, insight, generosity, compassion, and wonderful sense of humour. I cannot imagine writing this book on my own or with anyone else.

Brock University, its Humanities Research Institute, and its Centre for Pedagogical Innovation have been generous in their support.

I would like to thank my students over the many years for reminding me of the reasons I wanted to become a professor in the very first place.

I am grateful to all of my colleagues at Brock, in particular Robert Alexander, Lynn Arner, Leslie Boldt, Tim Conley, Keri

Cronin, Neta Gordon, Jill Grose, Ann Howey, Barry Joe, Leah Knight, Martin Danahay, Tanya Rohrmoser, Janet Sackfie, Elizabeth Sauer, and Joan Wiley for their interest in this project. Some of you sent me articles that made the book better. Thank you. Dennis Denisoff (Ryerson), Peter Sabor (McGill), and Wendy Shilton (University of Prince Edward Island) are great colleagues, except for the fact that they are not as close by as I'd like!

Thank you, Morgan Holmes, for your continued friendship and that ballroom dancing years ago, and for recommending to me Carl Honoré's *In Praise of Slow*.

And Frida and Georgie for reminding me all the time that there is life outside of the academy.

Works Cited

Ailamaki, Anastassia, and Johannes Gehrke. "Time Management for New Faculty." *SIGMOD Record* 32.2 (2003): 102–6.

Alves, Julio. "Unintentional Knowledge: What We Find When We're Not Looking." *Chronicle of Higher Education* 23 Jun. 2013. n.p. Web. 21 Feb. 2015. <http://chronicle.com/article/Unintentional-Knowledge/139891/>

Andrews, Cecile. *Slow Is Beautiful: New Visions of Community, Leisure and Joie de Vivre*. Gabriola Island, BC: New Society Publishers, 2006.

Andrews, Geoff. *The Slow Food Story: Politics and Pleasure*. Montreal & Kingston: McGill-Queen's University Press, 2008.

Aronowitz, Stanley. *The Knowledge Factory: Dismantling the Corporate University and Creating True Higher Learning*. Boston: Beacon Press, 2000.

Austen, Jane. *Northanger Abbey*. Ed. Barbara M. Benedict and Deidre Le Faye. Cambridge: Cambridge University Press, 2006.

Bakker, Arnold B., and Wilmar B. Schaufeli. "Burnout Contagion Processes among Teachers." *Journal of Applied Social Psychology* 30.11 (2000): 2289–308.

Barcan, Ruth. *Academic Life and Labour in the New University*. Burlington, VT: Ashgate, 2013.

Barry, Jim, John Chandler, and Heather Clark. "Between the Ivory Tower and the Academic Assembly Line." *Journal of Management Studies* 38.1 (2001): 87–101.

Barsade, Sigal G. "The Ripple Effect: Emotional Contagion and Its Influence on Group Behavior." *Administrative Science Quarterly* 47.4 (2002): 644–75.

Beard, Colin, Barbara Humberstone, and Ben Clayton. "Positive
    Emotions: Passionate Scholarship and Student Transformation."
    Teaching in Higher Education 19.6 (2014): 630–43.

Bekoff, Marc. "Wild Justice and Fair Play: Cooperation, Forgiveness,
    and Morality in Animals." *Animal Studies Reader.* Ed. Linda Kalof
    and Amy Fitzgerald. Oxford: Berg, 2007. 72–90.

Blackie, Margaret A.L., Jennifer M. Case, and Jeff Jawitz. "Student-
    Centredness: The Link between Transforming Students and Trans-
    forming Ourselves." *Teaching in Higher Education* 15.6 (2010): 637–46.

Boice, Robert. *Advice for New Faculty Members: Nihil Nimus.* Needham
    Heights, MA: Allen & Bacon, 2000.

– *First-Order Principles for College Teachers: Ten Basic Ways to Improve the
    Teaching Process.* Bolton, MA: Anker Pub. Co., 1996.

Brabazon, Tara. *The University of Google: Education in the (Post)
    Information Age.* Aldershot, Hampshire, England; Burlington, VT:
    Ashgate, 2007.

Brennan, Teresa. *The Transmission of Affect.* Ithaca: Cornell University
    Press, 2004.

Brooks, David. "The Waning of I.Q." *Pittsburgh Post-Gazette* 17 Sep.
    2007.

Brown, Brené. *The Gifts of Imperfection: Let Go of Who You Think You're
    Supposed to Be and Embrace Who You Are.* Center City: Hazelden, 2010.

Buckholdt, David R., and Gale E. Miller. "Conclusion: Is Stress
    Likely to Abate for Faculty?" *Journal of Human Behavior in the Social
    Environment* 17.1/2 (2008): 213–29.

Burrell, Amanda, and Michael Coe. "Be Quiet and Stand Still."
    Conference paper, ANZMAC 2007. Web. 21 Feb. 2015. <http://www
    .anzmac.org/conference_archive/2007/papers/A%20Burrell_1a
    .pdf>

Burrell, Amanda, Michael Coe, and Shaun Cheah. "Making an
    Entrance: The First Two Minutes Can Make or Break a Lecture."
    Conference paper, ANZMAC 2007. Web. 21 Feb. 2015. <http://
    www.anzmac.org/conference_archive/2007/papers/A%20Burrell_
    2a.pdf>

Cacioppo, John T., and Louise C. Hawkley. "Perceived Social Isolation
    and Cognition." *Trends in Cognitive Science* 13.10 (2009): 447–54.

Caine, Renate N., and Geoffrey Caine. *Education on the Edge of Possibility.* Alexandria, VA.: Association for Supervision and Curriculum Development, 1997.

CareerCast. "The 10 Least Stressful Jobs of 2013." Web. 25 Jul. 2015. <http://www.careercast.com/jobs-rated/10-least-stressful-jobs-2013>

– "The Least Stressful Jobs of 2014." Web. 25 Jul. 2015. <http://www.careercast.com/jobs-rated/least-stressful-jobs-2014>

Carr, Nicholas. *The Shallows: What the Internet Is Doing to Our Brains.* New York: Norton, 2010.

Catano, Vic, Lori Francis, Ted Haines, Haresh Kirpalani, Harry Shannon, Bernadette Stringer, and Laura Lozanksi. *Occupational Stress among Canadian University Academic Staff.* Canadian Association of University Teachers, 2007. Web. 21 Feb. 2015. <http://www.unbc.ca/sites/default/files/sections/si-transken/occupationalstressamongcanadianuniversity.doc>

Chatfield, Tom. *How to Thrive in the Digital Age.* London: Macmillan, 2012.

Coleman, Daniel, and Smaro Kamboureli. Coda. *Retooling the Humanities: The Culture of Research in Canadian Universities.* Ed. Coleman and Kamboureli. Edmonton: University of Alberta Press, 2011. 263–7.

– Preface. *Retooling the Humanities: The Culture of Research in Canadian Universities.* Ed. Coleman and Kamboureli. Edmonton: University of Alberta Press, 2011. xiii–xxiv.

Collini, Stefan. *English Pasts: Essays in Culture and History.* Oxford: Oxford University Press, 1999.

– *What Are Universities For?* London: Penguin, 2012.

Conti, R. "Time Flies: Investigating the Connection between Intrinsic Motivation and Time Awareness." *Journal of Personality* 69.1 (2001): 1–26.

Côté, James E., and Anton L. Allahar. *Ivory Tower Blues: A University System in Crisis.* Toronto: University of Toronto Press, 2007.

– *Lowering Higher Education: The Rise of Corporate Universities and the Fall of Liberal Education.* Toronto: University of Toronto Press, 2011.

Cipriano, Robert E., and Jeffrey L. Buller. "Rating Faculty Collegiality." *Change* 44.2 (2012): 45–8.

Crenshaw, Dave. *The Myth of Multitasking: How "Doing It All" Gets Nothing Done.* San Francisco: Jossey-Bass, 2008.

Csikszentmihalyi, Mihaly. *Flow: The Psychology of Optimal Experience.* New York: Harper Perennial Modern Classics, 2008.

Cuddy, Amy. TED: Ideas Worth Spreading. Podcast. Jun. 2012. Web. 21 Feb. 2015. <http://video.ted.com/talk/podcast/2012G/None/ AmyCuddy_2012G-480p.mp4>

Cuny, Janice. "Time Management and Family Issues." Web. 21 Feb. 2015. <http://math.mit.edu/wim/links/articles/timemanage.pdf>

Dabney, Jackie. "Stress in Students: Implications for Learning?" *Innovations in Education and Training International* 32.2 (1995): 112–16.

Damasio, Antonio R. *Descartes' Error: Emotion, Reason, and the Human Brain.* New York: Avon Books, G.P. Putnam, 1994.

Deresiewicz, William. "Faulty Towers: The Crisis in Higher Education." *Nation.* Web. 4 May 2011. <http://www.thenation.com>

Donoghue, Frank. *The Last Professors: The Corporate University and the Fate of the Humanities.* New York: Fordham University Press, 2008.

Edemariam, Aida. "Who's Afraid of the Campus Novel?" *Guardian* 2 Oct. 2004: 34.

Evans, James. A. "Electronic Publication and the Narrowing of Science and Scholarship." *Science* 321.5887 (2008): 395–9.

Fanghanel, Joëlle. *Being an Academic.* London: York: Routledge, 2012.

Franken, Al, writer and performer. *Stuart Saves His Family.* Dir. Harold Ramis. Paramount Pictures, 1995. Film.

Franklin, Adrian S. "On Loneliness." *Geografiska Annaler: Series B, Human Geography* 91.4 (2009): 343–54.

Fredrickson, Barbara L. "The Role of Positive Emotions in Positive Psychology: The Broaden-and-Build Theory of Positive Emotions." *American Psychologist* 56.3 (2001): 218–26.

Frisch, Jennifer Kreps, and Gerald Saunders. "Using Stories in an Introductory College Biology Course." *JBE: Journal of Biological Education* 42. 4 (2008): 164–9. Web. 21 Feb. 2015. <http://www .academia.edu/250488/ Using_Stories_In_An_Introductory_College_Biology_Course>

Ginsberg, Benjamin. *The Fall of the Faculty: The Rise of the All-Administrative University and Why It Matters.* Oxford: Oxford University Press, 2011.

Giroux, Henry A. "The Attack on Higher Education and the Necessity of Critical Pedagogy." *Critical Pedagogy in Uncertain Times: Hope and Possibilities.* Ed. Sheila L. Macrine. New York: Palgrave, 2009. 11–26.

— *Education and the Crisis of Public Values: Challenging the Assault on Teachers, Students, and Public Education.* New York: Peter Lang, 2012.

— *The University in Chains: Confronting the Military-Industrial-Academic Complex.* Boulder, CO: Paradigm, 2007.

— "Rejecting Academic Labor as a Subaltern Class: Learning from Paulo Freire and the Politics of Critical Pedagogy." *Fast Capitalism* 8.2 (2011). Web. 23 Jul., 2015.

Gmelch, Walter H. *Coping with Faculty Stress.* Newbury Park: Sage, 1993.

Hall, Donald E. *The Academic Community: A Manual for Change.* Columbus: Ohio State University Press, 2007.

— *The Academic Self: An Owner's Manual.* Columbus: Ohio State University Press, 2002.

Hall, Donald E., and Susan S. Lanser. "That Was Then, This Is Now, but What Will Be? A Dialogue between Two Generations of Professors." *Professions: Conversations on the Future of Literary and Cultural Studies.* Ed. Donald E. Hall. Chicago: University of Illinois Press, 2001. 203–23.

Hallowell, Edward M. *CrazyBusy: Overstretched, Overbooked, and about to Snap!* New York: Ballantine, 2007.

Hanson, Rick. *Hardwiring Happiness: The New Brain Science of Contentment, Calm, and Confidence.* New York: Harmony, 2013.

Harmgardt, Julie. "A Multitasker's Impossible Dream?" *Queen's Alumni Review* 4 (2012): 8–9.

Hassan, Robert. "Network Time and the New Knowledge Epoch." *Time & Society* 12.2/3 (2003): 225–41.

Heiberger, Morris Mary, and Julia Miller Vick. *The Academic Job Search Handbook.* 3rd. ed. Philadelphia: University of Pennsylvania Press, 2001.

Honoré, Carl. *In Praise of Slow: How a Worldwide Movement Is Challenging the Cult of Speed.* Toronto: Vintage, 2004.

Huston, Therese. *Teaching What You Don't Know.* Cambridge, Mass: Harvard University Press, 2009.

Hutcheon, Linda. "Saving Collegiality." *Profession* (2006) 60–4.

Jarvis, Donald K. *Junior Faculty Development: A Handbook.* New York: Modern Language Association, 1991.

Jönsson, Bodil. *Unwinding the Clock: Ten Thoughts on Our Relationship to Time.* Trans. Tiina Nunnally. San Diego: Harcourt, 2001.

Kahneman, Daniel. *Thinking, Fast and Slow.* Toronto: Anchor Canada, 2013.

Klusmann, Uta, Mareike Kunter, Ulrich Trautwein, Oliver Lüdtke, and Jürgen Baumert. "Teachers' Occupational Well-Being and Quality of Instruction: The Important Role of Self-Regulatory Patterns." *Journal of Educational Psychology* 100.3 (2008): 702–15.

Inspector Morse: The Last Enemy. Zenith Production for Central Independent Television, 1988.

Lewis, Harry R. "Slow Down: Getting More out of Harvard by Doing Less." Web. 21 Feb. 2015. <http://lewis.seas.harvard.edu/files/harrylewis/files/slowdown2004_0.pdf>

Lewis, Harry, and Philip Hills. *Time Management for Academics.* Little Fransham: Peter Francis, 1999.

Lewis, Magda. "More Than Meets the Eye: The Under Side of the Corporate Culture of Higher Education and Possibilities for a New Feminist Critique." *Journal of Curriculum Theorizing* 21.1 (2005): 7–25.

Lindholm, Jennifer A., and Katalin Szelényi. "Faculty Time Stress: Correlates within and across Academic Disciplines." *Journal of Human Behavior in the Social Environment* 17.1/2 (2008): 19–40.

Lodge, David. *Changing Places: A Tale of Two Campuses.* London: Penguin, 1978.

– *Deaf Sentence.* London: Harvill Secker, 2008.

Mackenzie, Alec. *The Time Trap: The Classic Book on Time Management.* New York, NY: AMACON, 1997.

Mainemelis, Charalampos. "When the Muse Takes It All: A Model for the Experience of Timelessness in Organisations." *The Academy of Management Review* 26.4 (2001): 548–65.

Martela, Frank. "Sharing Well-Being in a Work Community: Exploring Well-Being Generating Relational Systems." *Emotions and the Organizational Fabric. Research on Emotion in Organizations* 10 (2014): 79–110.

Massachusetts Institute of Technology. "Findings of the Faculty Survey Conducted in October 2001." MIT Quality of Life Survey. Web. 21 Feb. 2015. <http://hrweb.mit.edu/workfamily/pdf/fqol.pdf>

Menzies, Heather. *No Time: Stress and the Crisis of Modern Life.* Vancouver: Douglas & McIntyre, 2005.

Menzies, Heather, and Janice Newson. "No Time to Think: Academics' Life in the Globally Wired University." *Time & Society* 16.1 (2007): 83–98.

– "The Over-Extended Academic in the Global Corporate Economy." *CAUT/ACPPU Bulletin* 48.1 (2001). Web. 22 Jul 2015. <https://www.cautbulletin.ca/en_article.asp?ArticleID=1669>

Miller, Gale E., David R. Buckholdt, and Beth Shaw. "Introduction: Perspectives on Stress and Work." *Journal of Human Behavior in the Social Environment* 17.1/2 (2008): 1–18.

Nakadate, Neil. *Understanding Jane Smiley.* Columbia: University of South Carolina Press, 1999.

Nelson, Ian. *Time Management for Teachers.* London: Kogan Page, 1995.

Newson, Janice. "The University-On-The-Ground: Reflections on the Canadian Experience." *Reconsidering Knowledge: Feminism and the Academy.* Ed. Meg Luxton and Mary Jane Mossman. Halifax: Fernwood, 2012. 96–127.

Nussbaum, Martha C. *Not For Profit: Why Democracy Needs the Humanities.* Princeton: Princeton University Press, 2010.

O'Reilley, Mary Rose. *The Peaceable Classroom.* Portsmouth, NH: Boynton/Cook Publishers, 1993.

Orr, David W. *The Nature of Design: Ecology, Culture, and Human Intention.* Oxford: Oxford University Press, 2002.

Ostrow, Ellen. "Setting Boundaries in the Ivory Tower." *The Chronicle of Higher Education* 8 Sept. 2000. Web. 21 Feb. 2015. <http://chronicle.com/article/Setting-Boundaries-in-the-I/46372>

Palmer, Parker J. *The Courage to Teach: Exploring the Inner Landscape of a Teacher's Life.* San Francisco: Wiley Jossey-Bass, 1998.

Panksepp, Jaak. "The Riddle of Laughter: Neural and Psychoevolutionary Underpinnings of Joy." *Current Directions in Psychological Science* 9.6 (2000): 183–6.

Parker, Martin and David Jary. "The McUniversity: Organization, Management and Academic Subjectivity." *Organization* 2.2 (1995): 319–38.

Parkins, Wendy, and Geoffrey Craig. *Slow Living.* Oxford: Berg, 2006.

Paul, Annie Murphy. "Eight Ways of Looking at Intelligence." *The Brilliant Blog.* 10 Jun. 2013. Web. 21 Feb. 2015. <anniemurphypaul.com/2013/06/eight-ways-of-looking-at-intelligence>

Pennee, Donna Palmateer. "Taking it Personally and Politically: The Culture of Research in Canada after Cultural Nationalism." *Retooling the Humanities: The Culture of Research in Canadian Universities*. Ed. Daniel Coleman and Smaro Kamboureli. Edmonton: University of Alberta Press, 2011. 59–75.

Perullo, Nicola. "Slow Knowledge." *Slow* 57 (2007): 16–21.

Petrini, Carlo. *Slow Food: The Case for Taste*. New York: Columbia University Press, 2001.

– *Slow Food Nation: Why Our Food Should Be Good, Clean, and Fair*. Trans. Clara Furlan and Jonathan Hunt. New York: Rizzoli ex libris, 2007.

Philipson, Ilene. *Married to the Job: Why We Live to Work and What We Can Do about It*. New York: The Free Press, 2002.

Picard, R.W., S. Papert, W. Bender, B. Blumberg, C. Breazeal, D. Cavallo, T. Machover, M. Resnick, D. Roy, and C. Strohecker. "Affective Learning: A Manifesto." *BT Technology Journal* 22.4 (2004): 253–69.

Pocklington, T.C., and Allan Tupper. *No Place to Learn: Why Universities Aren't Working*. Vancouver: University of British Columbia Press, 2002.

Posen, David. *Is Work Killing You? A Doctor's Prescription for Treating Workplace Stress*. Toronto: Anansi, 2013.

Prichard, Craig, and Hugh Willmott. "Just How Managed Is the McUniversity?" *Organization Studies* 18.2 (1997): 287–316.

Queen's University at Kingston, Ontario. "Teaching and Learning Action Plan." Feb. 2014. Web. 21 Feb. 2015. <http://queensu.ca/provost/responsibilities/committees/s/TeachingAndLearningActionPlanMarch2014.pdf>

Readings, Bill. *The University in Ruins*. Cambridge: Harvard University Press, 1996.

Rettig, Hillary. *The Seven Secrets of the Prolific: The Definitive Guide to Overcoming Procrastination, Perfectionism, and Writer's Block*. 2011.

Robinson, Susan. *The Peak Performing Professor: A Practical Guide to Productivity and Happiness*. San Francisco: John Wiley and Sons, Jossey-Bass, 2013.

Ryan, Richard M., and Edward L. Deci. "Self-Determination Theory and the Facilitation of Intrinsic Motivation, Social Development, and Well-Being." *American Psychologist* 55.1 (2000): 68–78.

Sana, Faria, Tim Weston, and Nicholas J. Cepeda. "Laptop Multitasking Hinders Classroom Learning for Both Users and Nearby Peers." *Computers and Education* 62 (2013): 24–31.

Schaefer, Judith. "Truth through Glass: The Windows of *Moo*." *Notes on Contemporary Literature* 29.2 (1999): 3–4.

Schlosser, Eric. *Fast Food Nation: The Dark Side of the All-American Meal.* New York: Houghton Mifflin, 2001.

Scribendi Inc. (CA) "10 Time Management Techniques for Academics." 1997–2015. Web. 21 Feb. 2015. <https://www.scribendi.com/advice/10_time_management_techniques_for_academics.en.html>

Searle-White, Joshua, and Dan Crozier. "Embodiment and Narrative: Practices for Enlivening Teaching." *Transformative Dialogues* 5.2 (2011): 1–13.

Seldin, Peter, ed. *Coping with Faculty Stress.* San Francisco: Jossey Bass, 1987.

Semenza, Gregory Colón. *Graduate Study for the Twenty-First Century: How to Build an Academic Career in the Humanities.* New York: Palgrave MacMillan, 2005.

Shaw, Claire, and Lucy Ward. "Dark Thoughts: Why Mental Illness Is on the Rise in Academia." *Guardian Higher Education Network.* 6 Mar. 2014. Web. 21 Feb. 2015. <http://www.theguardian.com/higher-education-network/2014/mar/06/mental-health-academics-growing-problem-pressure-university>

Shenk, David. *Data Smog: Surviving the Information Glut.* San Francisco: Harper Collins, 1997.

– "The E Decade: Was I Right about the Dangers of the Internet in 1997?" *Slate Magazine* 25 Jul. 2007. Web. 26 Jul. 2007. <http://www.slate.com/articles/arts/culturebox/2007/07/the_e_decade.html>

Showalter, Elaine. *Teaching Literature.* Oxford: Blackwell Publishing, 2003.

Skovholt, Thomas M., and Michelle Trotter-Mathison. *The Resilient Practitioner: Burnout Prevention and Self-Care Strategies for Counselors, Therapists, Teachers, and Health Professionals.* New York and London: Routledge, 2011.

Slaughter, Sheila, and Larry L. Leslie. *Academic Capitalism: Politics, Policies, and the Entrepreneurial University.* Baltimore: Johns Hopkins University Press, 1997.

The Slow Science Academy. "The Slow Science Manifesto." 2010. Web. 21 Feb. 2015. <http://slow-science.org>

Smiley, Jane. *Moo.* New York: Fawcett Columbine, 1995.

Smith, Zadie. *NW.* London: Hamish Hamilton, 2012.

Solnit, Rebecca. "Finding Time: The Fast, the Bad, the Ugly, the Alternatives." *Orion Magazine*. Web. 21 Feb. 2015. <http://orionmagazine.org/article/a-fistful-of-time>

Swift, Jonathan. "Verses on the Death of Dr. Swift, D.S.P.D." *Jonathan Swift: Major Works*. Ed. Angus Ross and David Woolley. Oxford: Oxford University Press, 2003. 514–30.

Taylor, Mark C. "Speed Kills." *The Chronicle of Higher Education*. 20 Oct. 2014. Web. 21 Feb. 2015. <http://chronicle.com/article/Speed-Kills/149401>

Taylor, Shelley E. "Fostering a Supportive Environment at Work." *The Psychologist-Manager Journal* 11 (2008): 265–83.

Telpner, Meghan. *UnDiet: Eat Your Way to Vibrant Health*. Toronto: McClelland & Stewart, 2013.

theory.org. Web. 21 Feb. 2015. <https://www.theory.org>

Thomas, Maura Nevel. *Personal Productivity Secrets: Do What You Never Thought Possible with Your Time and Attention ... and Regain Control of Your Life*. Indianapolis, IN: John Wiley & Sons, 2012.

Thornton, Margaret. "Universities Upside Down: The Impact of the New Knowledge Economy." *Reconsidering Knowledge: Feminism and the Academy*. Ed. Meg Luxton and Mary Jane Mossman. Halifax: Fernwood, 2012. 76–95.

Three Minute Thesis (3MT). University of Queensland. Web. 21 Feb. 2015. <http://threeminutethesis.org>

Tompkins, Jane. "The Way We Live Now." *Change* 24.6 (1992): 12–19.

Tompkins, Jane, and Gerald Graff. "Can We Talk?" *Professions: Conversations on the Future of Literary and Cultural Studies*. Ed. Donald E. Hall. Chicago: University of Illinois Press, 2001. 21–36.

Turkle, Sherry. *Alone Together: Why We Expect More from Technology and Less from Each Other*. New York: Basic Books, 2011.

VanderWeele, Tyler J., Louise C. Hawkley, and John T. Cacioppo. "On the Reciprocal Association between Loneliness and Subjective Well-Being." *American Journal of Epidemiology* 176.9 (2012): 777–84.

Wankat, Phillip C. *The Effective, Efficient Professor: Teaching, Scholarship and Service*. Boston: Allyn and Bacon, 2002.

Washburn, Jennifer. *University Inc.: The Corporate Corruption of Higher Education*. New York: Basic Books, 2006.

Weaver, Richard L., and Howard W. Cotrell. "Ten Specific Techniques for Developing Humor in the Classroom." *Education* 108.2 (Winter 1987): 167–79.

Wilson, Robin. "Faculty Culture Is Fractured." *Chronicle of Higher Education* 59.40 (2013): A24–7.

Wilson, Robin. "The Ivory Sweatshop: Academe Is No Longer a Convivial Refuge." *The Chronicle of Higher Education* 56.41 (25 Jul. 2010). Web. 21 Feb. 2015. <http://chronicle.com/article/The-Ivory-Sweatshop-Academe/123641/>

Wright, Sarah L. "Organizational Climate, Social Support and Loneliness in the Workplace." *The Effect of Affect in Organizational Settings. Research on Emotion in Organizations* 1 (2005): 123–42.

Ylijoki, Oili-Helena, and Hans Mäntylä. "Conflicting Time Perspectives in Academic Work." *Time & Society* 12.1 (2003): 55–78.

Zhong, Chen-Bo, and Geoffrey J. Leonardelli. "Cold and Lonely: Does Social Exclusion Literally Feel Cold?" *Psychological Science* 19.9 (2008): 838–42.

Index